WHAT WORLD IS THIS?

WHAT WORLD IS THIS?

A Pandemic Phenomenology

JUDITH BUTLER

Columbia University Press

New York

Columbia University Press
Publishers Since 1893
New York   Chichester, West Sussex
cup.columbia.edu

Library of Congress Cataloging-in-Publication Data

Names: Butler, Judith, 1956– author.
Title: What world is this? : a pandemic phenomenology /
Judith Butler.
Description: New York : Columbia University Press, [2022] |
Includes bibliographical references and index.
Identifiers: LCCN 2022003670 (print) | LCCN 2022003671
(ebook) | ISBN 9780231208284 (hardback) | ISBN 9780231208291
(trade paperback) | ISBN 9780231557351 (ebook)
Subjects: LCSH: Life—History—21st century. |
Civilization—History—21st century. | COVID-19 (Disease) |
Phenomenology.
Classification: LCC BD435 .B89 2022 (print) | LCC BD435
(ebook) | DDC 128/.5—dc23/eng/20220603
LC record available at https://lccn.loc.gov/2022003670
LC ebook record available at https://lccn.loc.gov/2022003671

Columbia University Press books are printed
on permanent and durable acid-free paper.

Printed in the United States of America

Cover design: Julia Kushnirsky
Cover painting: Lee Krasner, *Still Life*, © 2022 The Pollock-
Krasner Foundation / Artists Rights Society (ARS), New York

CONTENTS

ACKNOWLEDGMENTS

I AM GRATEFUL to Joan Vergés Gifra at the Càtedra Ferrater Mora de Pensament Contemporani at Universitat de Girona in Catalunya for the invitation to give this work as a series of lectures in the late fall of 2020. I thank Arcadia Press in Catalunya for publishing this book first. I am particularly thankful to Begonya Saez Tajafuerce, Fina Birules, Denise Riley, and Howard Caygill for their critical and imaginative engagement with this work. I thank as well Jarrett Zigon and Jason Throop and "Team Phenomenology" for their very helpful comments as well as the European Graduate School for inviting me to reflect on these matters online with an audience in the early phases of the pandemic. I thank as well the staff at Columbia University Press, especially Wendy Lochner, and the Wylie Agency for their dedication to the project.

WHAT WORLD IS THIS?

INTRODUCTION

What if this present were the world's last night?
—John Donne

REGARDLESS OF where we have lived in recent times, we are all living under a new set of conditions created by the Covid-19 pandemic. I am not saying that the pandemic creates a single condition under which we all live, since the pandemic cannot be separated from prevailing social and ecological conditions. Yet the pandemic now configures those prevailing conditions, including the war against Ukraine, in a new way—the bodies clustered in shelters, in transportation vehicles, amassed at the border. Such unchosen proximities would doubtless look differently were the pandemic fully vanished. Other prevailing conditions include environmental destruction, poverty, racism, global inequalities, and social violence, including violence directed against women and LGBTQI+ people. In these continuing pandemic times, some of us have doubtless suffered acute losses, and others may be observing those losses from safer parts of the world, but all of us have been living in relation to ambient illness and death. Death and illness have been quite literally in the air, and we are often left not knowing how to mark and mourn those who have died. However differently we register this pandemic—and what it means to *register* it will prove important to what I have to say about the phenomenology of the senses—we do doubtless understand it as global; it implicates each of us in an interconnected world, a world of living creatures whose capacity to affect one another, and to be affected by one another, can be a matter of life or death. I am not sure I would say that this is *a common world* we share since, as much as we might wish to dwell in a common world, it does not seem that we do. The common has not yet been achieved. Perhaps it is more apt to say that there are many and overlapping worlds, for so many of the major resources of the world are not equitably shared, and there remain those who have only a small or vanished share of the world. We cannot register a global phenomenon such as the pandemic without at once registering those inequalities and, in this time, seeing those inequalities intensify. We sometimes say that those with wealth and protection live in a different world than those who do not. That is a figure of speech, but does it not also communicate a reality? Maybe we ought not to be taken seriously when we speak that way if there is, after all, a singular world that encompasses such inequalities. But what if it remains descriptively true that some worlds are not quite part of that one world, that common world, or that there are zones of life that exist and persist outside the common or the commons?[1]

Often those who dwell in such marginal zones do the work for that common world and are tied to it through labor but are not for that reason *of* it, if by "of it" we mean to designate a mode of belonging. Indeed, perhaps those who constitute replaceable labor or who dwell outside the zone of productivity as recognized by capitalist metrics are considered the refuse, the waste of the common world, or its zone of criminality, Black and brown life, sometimes living in debt—living, in fact, in the endless time of unpayable debt, a debt that suffuses life and survives the life of the debtor. So maybe we need to think about contiguous and overlapping worlds that are uncommon or even, as Fred Moten and Stefano Harney argue, belong to an underlying "undercommons"—that is, a zone of negligence and criminality but also of refuge, experiments in community and art, and acts of affirmation often undertaken without sufficient funding.[2] If, in light of all this, we still want to talk about a shared or common world, we might, with Jacques Rancière, talk about "the part of those who have no part"—those for whom participation in the commons is not possible, never was, or no longer is.[3] If we were to talk about shares of the world—not financial shares but part of the common share that is the world—we would have to admit that there is no equitable measure for distributing equal shares of the world. A share would be a form of participation and belonging that could not be grasped by economic metrics and would doubtless demand a measure beyond that metric. For we are not just talking about resources and companies in which one could own a share of stock but a common world, a sense of the common, a sense of belonging to a world, or a sense of the world itself as a site of belonging. That is not the same, I think, as a struggle for recognition within the existing social coordinates and categories, for it entails a fundamental transformation of the understanding of value. As such, it is a way of living life with the assumptions that one's life has value—a value beyond market value—that the world will be structured to facilitate one's flourishing and that this happens, or will happen, not only for oneself but for everyone else as well.

We are, of course, far from any idea of a common world. The pandemic, and now the distribution of vaccines, illuminates and intensifies racial inequalities. A large portion of pandemic pain is clustered in some parts of the subjugated and colonized world and in communities of color. In the United States, Black and brown people have been three times as likely to become infected with the virus as white people, and twice as likely to die.[4] The statistics cannot explain how it got to be that way, but we can assume that one reason is that within the so-called common world the loss of Black life is simply not considered as worrisome or grievable as the loss of white life (often described simply as "human life"). Indeed, face to face with such statistical inequalities, we may find ourselves asking, *what kind of world is it in which those statistics emerge?* We can mean several things by such a question. We may be asking, *what version of reality do those statistics serve?* Or *what world is circumscribed by the statistics themselves?* Yet, even as social and economic inequalities are brought into fuller relief under pandemic conditions and as a growing and vulnerable undercommons of abandonment, fugitivity, and experimental life is exposed, there is also a movement in a global direction, one that seems based on a renewed and more acute sense of mortality coupled with a political sense of who dies early, whose death is preventable, whose death matters. For which set of living beings are there no safeguards, no infrastructural or social promise of continuity, no sense of a life with the supports required to live on? And now we see the global distribution of the vaccine and the grim reality that countries that cannot pay have yet to see a single dose.[5] The draw toward a global sense of the world (and let us presume that a global sense of the world is registered phenomenologically through different senses of the global) is strengthened by a common immunological predicament, even as it is one that we live out very differently depending on where we are and how we are socially positioned, if we are "positioned" at all within the operative sense of society.

Pandemic is etymologically *pan-demos*, all the people, or perhaps more precisely, the people everywhere, or something that crosses over or spreads over and through the people. It establishes the people as porous and interconnected. The *demos* is thus not the citizens of a given state but all the people despite the legal barriers that seek to separate them or their documented status. A pandemic operates throughout the world population, but it also afflicts the people as human creatures who bear a susceptibility to viral infection. "The world" that is implied is the everywhere, the *pan*, a world that is threaded together through infection and recovery, by immunity, differential risk, morbidity, and fatality. There is no border that stops the virus from traveling if humans travel, and no social category secures absolute immunity. Indeed, the pretense of power that acts as if some are immune by virtue of their social power increases the vulnerability to infection since it throws precautions to the wind, as we see with Jair Bolsonaro in Brazil and as we surely saw in lurid detail with the president of the United States who preceded Biden. The defiance of the "anti-vaxxers" intensifies their susceptibility and their risk of hospitalization and death, as we saw with the Delta and Omicron surges. It is as if the pandemic keeps insisting on the *pan*, drawing attention to the world, and the world keeps dividing into unequally exposed zones. So even though we tend to speak of the world as a singular horizon or even expect that the word *world* will set the horizon to experience itself, we also talk about *worlds* in the plural to highlight discontinuity, barriers, and inequalities, and we feel it is imperative to do so to describe the world as it is. Oddly, we don't generally hear about *worlds of the virus*, but we surely could in a provisional way. If we did, that would suggest that multiple world horizons are operative, horizons that do not always exactly fuse as Hans-Georg Gadamer expected them to; they would be asynchronous horizons, world-limits, as it were, configured through different temporalities that overlap and diverge but do not fully converge into a single one.[6]

Some have thought that we need to shake this notion of the world and turn to the planetary as a decidedly less anthropocentric concept. The planetary can furnish a critical perspective on geographical maps that are invariably geopolitical, whose lines are the accomplishments of those who vanquish, national boundaries usually forged through war or colonization. Achille Mbembe argues, "The political in our time must start from the imperative to reconstruct the world in common."[7] However, he argues, if we consider the plundering of the earth's resources for the purposes of corporate profit, privatization, and colonization itself as planetary project or enterprise, then it makes sense that the true opposition, the one that does not send us back to our egos, our barriers, and identities, will be a form of "decolonisation [that] is by definition a planetary enterprise, a radical openness of and to the world, *a deep breathing* for the world as opposed to insulation."[8] The planetary opposition to extractivism and systemic racism ought to then deliver us back to the world, or let the world arrive as if for the first time, in a way that allows for a "deep breathing"—a desire we all now know, if we have not already forgotten how to wish for it.

There are, of course, many ways to approach this question of the world, including the now complicated debates about "world" literature.[9] Sometimes there we find distinctions like "European" literature and "world" literature, as if the world is every other place outside of Europe or the Anglo-American context. In other words, the center of the world gets a place name, but all those other locations of literature are elsewhere and, therefore, the world. A vast domain and without proper names, the world becomes an elsewhere in relation to the centers of power. In contrast, the important work of decolonial feminist María Lugones, who in 1987 wrote on "world-travelling," offers a counterimperialist account of moving from one's own world to another's world in order to undergo a transformation in the direction of a more loving perception of alterity.[10] That work is now more than thirty years old yet continues to address readers across the world at the same time that it marks those separated worlds, underscoring the risk of disorientation in encountering another world, another language, or epistemic field. Lugones underscores the importance of letting one's epistemic field—one's very sense of the limit and structure of the world—become upended and reoriented in the course of an encounter in which one becomes willing to suspend or forfeit the coordinates of the world one has known in an effort to reach and apprehend another.

The pandemic has brought with it this oscillation between world and worlds. Whereas some insist that the pandemic intensifies all that was already wrong with the world, others suggest that the pandemic opens us to a new sense of global interconnection and interdependency. Both propositions are wagers that emerge amid a continuing contemporary disorientation. The pandemic distributes itself in waves and surges, and those correlate phenomenologically with hope and despair. No matter how located and differentiated the ways that pandemic registers for people across the world, it remains understood as a phenomenon, a force, a crisis, that extends throughout the world and that, considered as a condition of the present world, figures the world (or gives forth the world) in some quite specific ways. In other words, no one, no matter where they are, is not thinking about the world. Although some nations (like the United States under Donald Trump) reverted to hypernationalist frameworks for understanding the virus and its effects and even competed with the rest of the world to monopolize vaccinations, their efforts nevertheless index the interconnected world in some way. And though some regions seem to have escaped the worst ravages of the coronavirus by chance or have contained its effect through deliberate forms of social conduct, no region is in principle immune. No region, no bounded entity, indeed, no discrete body is by definition immune in advance.[11] For a pandemic names a global susceptibility, a potential suffering, that belongs to human life in its immunological relationship to the world, one that is part of the world for now and perhaps for an indefinite period of time. Once the virus becomes endemic, it will be an enduring part of the world. Interestingly, we do not have a noun for that: "there is an endemic unleashed on the world"—no, a pandemic can be unleashed, but an illness that is considered endemic becomes part of the fabric of the world itself, the experience of the world, a new sense of the world when all the unleashing has come to an end. It moves from noun to adjective, from a temporary condition of the world to a permanent feature. But even if this pandemic were to fade away, immunological vulnerability certainly will not. And if we hate the virus for the vulnerability it exposes, we ought not for that reason conclude that the absence of the virus will eradicate that vulnerability. Immunologically considered, the vulnerability foregrounded by the virus is a function of the fact that the exogenous is always a part of any organism: animals, including human ones, ingest, absorb, and breathe elements of an external world in order to live. In this way the human body, to live, can never be sealed off from what is external. Its life resides in the interaction with externality. This position articulated by co-constructionists such as Thomas Pradeu has implications for how we think about danger.[12] The problem with the virus is not that it is *foreign* but that it is *new*, and that is why our immunological systems, or most of ours, have no ready way to recognize it and to fight against it without the assistance of vaccines or antibodies (and T cells) that come to recognize it through exposure. The thesis of co-constructionists is that the organism is constructed by its environment even as it constructs that environment in return. (We see a version of this theory in Anne Fausto-Sterling's work as well, with important implications for reformulating the implications of the sex/gender distinction for the nature/culture distinction.[13]) The aim of a co-constructionist theory is less to distinguish what belongs to the self and what does not than to understand how the external world is part of the body—and has to be. Thus, the immunological problem produced by pandemics is an unpreparedness for what is unprecedented. Of course, if there were no analogies to other epidemics produced by SARS viruses, then the adenovirus vaccines would have been declared useless from the start. And messenger RNA vaccines, which seek to mimic the shape and spike of the virus, producing a new object-shape for the immune system through a life-saving simulacrum, are crucial to developing the immunological capacity to identify, react, and fight it. Both types of vaccines rely on the possibility of recognizing and reacting to a similar structure. Both analogy and mimicry are crucial to strengthening the immune system in this context. At the same time, however, the immune system is challenged not only by what comes from outside but also by the organism itself, which is why autoimmune attacks, those waged by the organism against itself, are very often the inflammatory consequence of new forms of viral infections. I underscore this point because at the outset of the pandemic, the virus was figured by media reports as coming from a place, a "foreign" place—China, Brazil, South Africa—and described as an unwanted immigrant, imported without proper papers into the body politic, at which point "public health" within the U.S. nation-state, for instance, was said to be imperiled by what is foreign. That was, and remains, more of an immigration analogy within a nationalist imaginary than an immunological model on which anyone can rely. I underscore this point because, as we know, the organism cannot survive without ingesting or taking in foreign elements. One is tempted to conclude that the organism can be more acutely at risk from its autoimmune condition than from anything foreign. But once we accept the co-constructionist model that establishes the foreign at the heart of the living organism and that prioritizes the inter-action between body and world as the life of the body itself, then the point is not to defend oneself against what is foreign—that would be fatal. Rather, the aim is to transform the interaction so that the body can live with and accommodate what is new with-out risk of debilitation or death.[14] The world is not just out there as the backdrop for human action or the field for human inter-vention; on a daily basis, bits of the world are incorporated into the body itself, suggesting a vital connection between body and world. This can have devastating effects when toxic air affects and degrades the lungs, when lead in water becomes part of the bones, when environmental poisons enter and imperil the body in its tissues and ligaments. The point is not to negate the exter-nal environment—that is an impossibility. The point is to clear the air and water of toxins so that living creatures may rely upon them without fear of the mortal consequences.

■ ■ ■

Call me a Lucretian, if you must, but we won't be able to under-stand shared vulnerability and interdependency unless we concede that we pass the air we breathe to one another, that we share the surfaces of the world, and that we cannot touch another without also being touched. We lose sight of that overlapping and reciprocity when, for instance, we forget that being infected and becoming infectious are linked together. What happens to me happens to another, at least potentially. This link between us can be fatal, but it can also, surely, be life-sustaining as well. The pandemic upends our usual sense of the bounded self, casting us as relational, interactive, and refuting the egological and self-interested bases of ethics itself.

I turn to phenomenology, and especially the work of Max Scheler, to understand better the ordinary language instance I referenced above: a question often now uttered in anguish or surprise: *what kind of a world is this in which such a thing like this can happen!?* But let me first make some preliminary remarks about the contexts in which such an enunciation appears. It may emerge because I am living in the aftermath of a regime that happily destroyed democratic institutions in a daily way or because my region is subject to massively destructive fires as the result of climate change, or because white supremacists are on the rise and congregating near or on campus, and because all of this happens within the context of a pandemic that continues to surge and strike in different regions and for different populations after periods of relative abeyance. I would suggest that the question *what kind of world is this?* seeks to fathom the world in which such a virus can happen. It is not just that the virus is new but that the world is now exhibited or disclosed as a different sort of world than we once thought it was (those who, for instance, were not subject to Ebola in recent history). An aspect of the world is transformed by the emergence of the virus and its effects. Of course, I would not argue that what emerges now is an altogether new idea of the world since pandemics have happened before, and the world was always a place where pandemics could happen, or so it has seemed for several centuries. I am suggesting only that something about the pandemic makes us reconsider the world as an object of scrutiny, register the world as a cause for alarm, mark the fact that this present version of the world was not anticipated, and see the world as suddenly bearing a new kind of opacity and imposing a new set of constraints.

Ludwig Wittgenstein wrote that one should not confuse one's will with the world that is given, implicitly refuting the Schopenhauerian recommendation that the world be understood as a representation. In the *Tractatus Logico-Philosophicus* (1921), Wittgenstein wrote a line that could easily be read as an alibi for quietism and positivism: "If good or bad willing changes the world, it can only change the limits of the world, not the facts; not the things that can be expressed in language."[15] At the time, he understood that the logic of language maintained a mimetic relationship to the structure of reality (later he turned to a notion of language as a language game and then as a form of life). What we will does have the power change *the limits* of the world, what we might understand as the horizon within which the world appears, its defining limit. In his view, something about the world can be represented by language in a way we had not seen before, which means that the world as a whole appears as different or "waxes" in the sense that the structure of reality proves to be different. When it is possible that our will, something we will, shifts the limits of the world, then the world becomes a new world. The line that follows suggests that this waxing of the world in its entirety is not the effect or representation of our will but, rather, the revelation of the world as a different world than we thought it was. Something we willed might have made that revelation possible, but what is then shown, what appears, is not therefore the simple effect of our will but, rather, a newer sense of the world, if not a newer world. Thus, he is not speaking about a single sense of the world that binds all living humans but successive senses of *world* that follow upon each other in time or that are, presumably, spatially distributed across the earth. Indeed, when the world admits of a new sense, the kind of sense that changes the limits of the world, which would include the sense of the limit, the world itself becomes a different world. It is no longer the world that we thought we lived in. In such cases, the limits of the presently constituted world are shifted, which means that the world becomes new. Wittgenstein puts it this way: "In brief, the world must thereby become quite another. It must so to speak wax or wane as a whole."[16] Perhaps offered as a tangent or as an example of his previous claim, he then writes, "the world of the happy is quite another than that of the unhappy."[17] Here he suggests that happiness is the kind of thing, along with the will, that can shift the limits of the world. Unhappiness as well, for the world appears as a different world from the perspective of unhappiness. It is the whole of the world that is implicated by happiness or unhappiness.

When we ask the question *what kind of world is this in which such a pandemic could happen?*, we are noting precisely such a shift. We stand, as it were, at the limit of the world we knew and pose the question from that precipice. In so asking about the world, taking the world as our object, in seeing that the world has taken us up in a new way, we no longer know the world and recognize that something has been disclosed to us that shifts our understanding of what the world is and how its limits are defined and registered. Perhaps one moved through the world without understanding that world to be a place where a potentially fatal viral infection could take place because of a chance encounter. Or one had that knowledge but figured it always happened elsewhere—a First World presumption. Now that we know that the world can be such a place (and people who have lived with epidemics have surely known that the world is such a place but maybe not *this* place), we have a different sense of the world. Perhaps it is not a new world, a new epoch, but rather the exhibition of something that was always latent in the world that only some of us have encountered. In this sense, something is exhibited as a feature of the world and not an effect of our perception. What is exhibited affects our perception, and even irreversibly affects our perception of the world.

The world the virus discloses or makes more clearly manifest—and unevenly permeates—cannot be conveyed adequately by a map or a picture, for this is something that is exhibited in the course of viral circulation and its effects. Of course, we may be given graphic pictures of the virus with its blue crown and spikes, and when these representations fill our screens, they stand in for—and still—a viral condition that they cannot adequately represent. They are closer to the logo of the virus, analogous to an advertisement for Disney World. The pictures function as abbreviated graphic forms that take the virus out of the quick and invisible time of its action and circulation, splash it with color, distill its spikes as a crown, enforcing a sense of clownish sovereignty. Although the once daily graphs and maps that seek to produce a picture of the viral world are surely useful, they provide a skewed understanding of the pandemic character of the virus by virtue of the pictorial form. Martin Heidegger claimed that "the world picture" is not a picture of the world but, rather, the world conceived and grasped as a picture.[18] He raised questions about whether the world could or should be conceived that way and what it meant that pictures were coming to stand for the world. He pointed out that the subject who stands before such a world picture seeks not only to grasp that visual version of the world in its entirety but finds itself exempt from the world it seeks to know.[19] Sometimes we find that conceit operating in the media, and it consoles us by presuming that we ourselves are not part of the picture that we see. And yet the effort to grasp the virus in pictorial or graphic terms does not actually secure the immunity of the perceiving subject. We are in the picture that we see, and the distance established by spectatorship is one that denies or at least suspends what it means to be implicated in the phenomenon that one seeks to know.

Does this sense of being implicated change, though, once we understand the viral world, or the sense of the world given by the virus, as one that pertains to touch and to breathing, to proximity and to distance as it works in invisible ways to produce existential effects? Part of what makes it frightening is that we cannot see it in everyday life without a rather powerful technological instrument, and the vast majority of us cannot understand its working without a popular translation from the fields of immunology and epidemiology. The vast majority of us have been left with anxious inference. Do you have it? Where is it? How do you know? We are left to understand the complicated and unprecedented character of this pandemic within the terms of our everyday lives. And this is made all the more difficult when governments and health ministries change their minds or turn out to be influenced by political or economic considerations when they announce public health decisions. We also know that what we must understand implicates us and everyone else existentially; that is, our knowing about the pandemic is a matter of life and death—and a shift in our very understanding of the world.

What field of study takes "the world" as its object? I suppose we could make a case for geography, astronomy, world literature, systems theory, environmental science. As someone trained in philosophy, I am drawn back to phenomenology, or perhaps compelled to draw it forward in order to understand the phenomenon of the pandemic as exhibiting a sense of world, or a world that is given to us in part through the senses.

Chapter 1

SENSES OF THE WORLD

SCHELER AND MERLEAU-PONTY

ONE TEXT that considers this sudden exhibition of the world in a new way is "On the Phenomenon of the Tragic," which Max Scheler published in German in 1915, the same year that Sigmund Freud published his *Reflections on War and Death* and the second year of the First World War.[1] The text belongs to the field of phenomenological research, which takes as its aim the study of the field of appearances. But it works in a heterodox way with Husserlian phenomenology, taking distance from those who would center phenomenological analysis in the subject and the question: what, and how, can a subject know what it knows. Edmund Husserl had opened up a debate within the field, one that became stronger in the 1930s through the 1950s about whether the correlations between the subjective and objective worlds (called noetic and noematic correlates) should emphasize one pole rather than the other. Is there a transcendental subject who constitutes the world from its own a priori structures, or does the world impose itself on our perception in ways that suggest that the ego and the subject are, in fact, superfluous? Ludwig Landgrebe, a German philosopher, made a strong case in the inaugural issue of *Philosophy and Phenomenological Research* in 1940 that the subject is the constitutive origin of the world, and that constituting the world is not the same as thematizing the world.[2] Although we are each born into an already constituted world, phenomenology asks us to bracket that world as we ask about its origins. The question of the origin of the world is not, for Landgrebe, a question of causality or creation but rather one of *constitution*, and for that there has to be a horizon, a line or a limit within which the world appears. What is worldly, that is, what belongs to or is *of* the world, appears within a pre-given horizon at the same time that it must be constituted as an appearance through a transcendental subjectivity. Landgrebe may not have had Scheler in mind since Jean-Paul Sartre had already in 1937 put forth his proposition to transcend the ego altogether, and, even earlier, numerous Husserlians, such as Aron Gurwitsch, were arguing that perhaps there is no transcendental ego or subject but only, at best, a transcendental field.[3] Husserl himself maintained in his *Phenomenology of Internal Time Consciousness* that the world appears for a consciousness as valid through a series of steps, a temporalization (*Zeitigung*).[4] In turn, the world subjectively takes shape as valid for us only within a temporal horizon and, thus, as a temporal succession. The world constituting power of consciousness neither creates nor establishes the world but answers to the question: *under what conditions does the world appear to us such that we might know it?* Through what temporal sequence, and in relation to what acts of knowing? In other words, the phenomenological doctrine of *constitution* is less an idealist conceit than an inquiry into how the world appears and how the world in its givenness takes shape in ways that are valid. For it is not enough to point to the world as the given horizon of experience and knowledge. If it is given, it has become given through a set of processes and acts that in no way dispute or minimize its given character, its objectivity—even the objective must appear in some way to be known.

Writing twenty-five years earlier, Scheler was deeply influenced by Husserl but was not convinced that Husserl's philosophy supported objective reality, including objective features of the world. The essay treats the tragic as a kind of phenomenon that can be treated on its own. It has an objective status as a noematic cluster, as the Husserlians might say. The tragic, however, is not primarily constituted by human consciousness or acts of projection or interpretation, or as the direct result of human actions. In this way, Scheler offers a means to think about the tragic that clearly departs from an Aristotelian understanding of tragic action according to which a dire set of consequences unfolds consistent with rules of likelihood and probability. The tragic, for Scheler, is not regulated by rules. Oddly, the tragic is found neither in the character of a play nor as an exclusively aesthetic problem; it neither defines a genre nor a character with a flaw, brought down by moral blindness or weakness. Scheler's text surprises with its suggestion that we consider the tragic as a way in which the world exhibits itself. Yes, the tragic appears by virtue of human events, but it is not the specificity of the human that it shows. Rather, it is a feature of the world, one of its qualities. "The tragic," he writes,

> is above all a property [*ein Merkmal*] which we observe in events, fortunes, characters, and the like, and which actually exists in them. *We might say that it is given off by them like a heavy breath* [*ein schwerer, kuehler Hauch, der von diesen Dingen selbst ausgeht*], or seems like an obscure glimmering that surrounds them. In it a specific feature of the world's makeup appears before us, and not a condition of our own ego, nor its emotions, nor its experience of compassion and fear.[5]

If we doubted whether his essay could speak to us in pandemic times, consider that, in addition to the heavy breath, the tragic depends on aerobic emanations that come from elsewhere just like the virus—leading one to speculate whether the tragic has viral character, moving and encircling as a virus does. It is a heavy breath that gives off something, and some lingering aerobic traces are apparently illuminated by a special kind of light.

Although Scheler sought to establish the objectivity of a wide range of phenomena that I find implausible, including "a hierarchy of values," I do find it interesting that this term, *the tragic*, has an objective aura in his writing. Although the tragic comes about by virtue of events, it is not itself an event. At most, on Scheler's account, it is a category under which certain kinds of experiences are gathered. He draws our attention to a relatively simple formulation: "to belong to the category of the tragic some value must be destroyed."[6] I take it that the kind of value destroyed in "the tragic," demonstrated by "the tragic," is one that is difficult to imagine as destructible. What is that value? Or how might that set of values be circumscribed? The tragic is not the same as a sadness that knows and names what it is sad about. When we speak about tragic grief, in his view, it "contains a definite composure" or sense of peace.[7] And, importantly, it extends *beyond the horizon* of the world—a formulation that departs from Husserl's philosophy. The tragic is less a consequence of our own action than the result of something arriving from the outside and subsequently permeating the soul—his phrase. Even as the tragic is occasioned by *events*—what come to be understood as tragic events—the tragic can never be reduced to the event which is its occasion; it persists, rather, as a kind of atmosphere (*geistige Atmosphaere*) in which an uncompromising and inevitable destruction of a value takes place.[8] In this way, although the tragic event is an occasion for the tragic, something more is exhibited, namely, a set of components that, taken together, constitute "the very makeup of the world." These are the components, Scheler writes, that "make such a thing possible."[9] In other words, the event exhibits something about the world: the event is its occasion, but the world is at once its condition and the phenomenon itself: "the tragic is always concerned with what is individual, singular, but at the same time, the constitution of the world itself [*eine Konstitution der Welt selbst*]."[10] So it is clearly not the case, for Scheler, that the world is constituted by a transcendental subject, not even in the qualified sense that Husserl offered. Rather, on the occasion of great loss and destruction of something or someone valuable or, perhaps more precisely, some value that they bear, the tragic emerges, consisting not only in the grief over that loss but the shock or bewilderment that the world is such that an event like that could happen at all.

My wager is that Scheler names this sense of the tragic residing in the exclamatory fragment "what kind of world is this in which such a thing can happen!"; it is not just *this* event, *this* loss, or the destruction of *this* value but the world in which such a destruction is possible or, perhaps, the world in which such a destruction has become possible. The wager of Scheler's intense antisubjectivism is that in or through the tragic event, "we are directly confronted with a definite condition of the world's makeup without deliberation or any sort of 'interpretation.'"[11] Here is the longer version of his argument:

This confronts us in the event itself; it does not result from what it does to the things which brought it about. It is only momentarily connected with the event and is independent of the elements that make it up. . . . The depth is brought about by the fact that its subject is twofold. One is the element of the event that has been seen by us. The other is that point in the world's makeup [constitution] that is exemplified by the event and of which the event is but an example. Grief seems to pour out from the event into unlimited space [beyond the horizon of the world]. It is not a universal, abstract world-makeup [constitution] that would be the same in all tragic events. It is rather a definite, individual element of the world's construction. The remote subject of the tragic is always the world itself, the world taken as a whole which makes such a thing possible. This "world" itself seems to be the object immersed in sorrow.[12]

The text suggests that the point is precisely not to say, "oh the loss of this or that life is not important, but only the loss of a sense of *world* in which those events remained unimaginable." No, it is about the life and the world in which such a life has lived. It is both at once. It is the movement between the two. The sorrow, in fact, moves between life and world, the event of loss, singular and irreversible, and the world, now in its unpicturable entirety immersed in sorrow. In some ways this is true insofar as the stories of loss overlap: the cell phone at the hospital; the getting barred at the hospital door; the inability to get to a hospital or to get close to the one who is dying. They refer to this loss and that loss, each very specific loss, and yet as the mode of reference repeats across its occasions, a looming world of loss emerges, or perhaps its ambient atmosphere becomes, or threatens to become, the air itself, or the very way that the air is registered here and now. We breathe, and that means we are alive in some sense. But if potential and actual grief is in the air we breathe, then the breath is now the means of passage for the virus and for the grief that sometimes follows, as well as the life that survives.

But Scheler suggest that, with the tragic, some very positive value is destroyed. What is that value? What are those values? One value is touch. The other is breath. Another is the complex surfaces and enclosures of the world—the infrastructure of habitation, figured both as shelter and refuge but also as a potentially dangerous enclosure. I am hardly saying anything new when I make the normative claim that the world of surfaces and the air we breathe should function as supports for life itself. Under pandemic conditions, the very elements upon which we depend for life carry the potential to take life: we come to worry about touching someone, and breathing their air, unexpected proximity, loud shouts of joy or vibrant song emanating from a stranger, dancing too closely. All that is a drag, something that drags us down, a kind of perpetual sorrow that afflicts all the joints of sociality. Taking Scheler as a point of departure, then, I want to ask more about how to live a life under such conditions and, more generally, ask about the conditions of a livable life. It is as if the basic requirements for life have been laid bare, and we become aware of the easier, less self-conscious ways of touching and breathing that we perhaps had before. We lose the kinds of proximity that we valued; we lose touch, tactility as a sense, and connection. We recede behind boundaries, if we have them and can afford them, of selfhood and space, of shelter and household, of neighborhood paths, as the value of extra-domestic intimacy and sociality is lost, as we lose touch across the enforced distances.

It is of course this or that loved person, or this or that kind of gathering, that we have surely missed, but it is also the constriction of the horizon that delimits what we call the world. So perhaps the problem is not only the one that Scheler specifies as tragic—the world in which such viral threat and destruction is possible—but also the question of life: *what does it mean to live as a living creature, a creature among creatures, a life among living processes, under conditions such as these?* He mentions a kind of guilt that is associated with the tragic, but it is not one that leads back to the actions of the individual. It is, rather, a sense of responsibility that emerges, it seems, from the structure of the world itself, from the fact that we are responsible for one another even though we cannot hold ourselves personally responsible for creating the conditions and instruments of harm. In his words, "The tragic consists—at least in human tragedies—not simply in the absence of 'guilt' but rather in the fact that the guiltiness cannot be localized."[13] In fact, the sense of the tragic increases as it becomes impossible to pin point the blame for events.

The restrictions are, of course, occasions for new experimentations—communities of care that are not bound by households—that establish kin beyond the nuclear and normative family. But there is also the sense that a partially stopped economy gave the environment a chance to renew and repair even as more people required packaged deliveries often filled with plastics. Strangers have treated each other not only with paranoia but also with remarkable solicitude. Social movements, like Black Lives Matter, have taken to the streets in masks and acted in responsible enough ways so that no spikes in the virus could be traced to those impressive and ongoing actions for racial and economic justice.[14] The case for national health care has never seemed stronger where I live; the possibility of hearing the case for guaranteed national income and single-payer health care is now more possible than before. Socialist ideals are renewed. And the movements to abolish prisons and defund the police are no longer "crazy" pipe dreams, as opponents would claim, but are openly debated in city councils and regional authorities followed by concrete actions to find alternatives to violent carceral institutions. And there is some form of grief and solidarity that crosses the social and economic lines that so often tend to separate human creatures from one another and impose hierarchies of value on them. Those who insist on denying the death, the loss, the stunning forms of economic and social inequality, have lost power as increasing numbers get vaccinated and accept mask-wearing as an obligation of public life.

The pandemic condition links us, establishing our ties as both precarious and persistent. The metric that tells us which lives are worth safeguarding and which lives are not is there to be seen and opposed, as is the metric that establishes acceptable levels of death—universities and businesses have made such determinations even as they deny that they do. Schools and universities have opened during pandemic peaks based on a calculation that only so many will fall ill and only so many will die. There is always a dispensable population factored into such equations. There are always people who can be sacrificed to make such equations work. And such decisions to open amid pandemic peaks indirectly target Black and brown people, the elderly, those with preexisting health conditions, the poor, the homeless, those with disabilities, and the incarcerated, including those stalled at the border or confined in overpopulated detention camps. In opposition to all these forms of destitution, there are new and renewed mobilizations, and they may be gaining in strength and number. They are each appalled by the world as it is currently constituted and endeavor to constitute a different kind of world. Yet it is not fully within their power to make the world anew, for human action is not at the center of the world. But a newer world does emerge once the conditions and limits to human action are established. Only then can climate destruction be reversed, and the ethical bonds between us set limits to self-aggrandizement and the economic calculations that accept the dispensability of those most vulnerable.

The question *what kind of world is this?* is prompted by another question: *how are we to live in this world?* And then perhaps a further set of questions follow: Given this world, what makes for a livable life? And what makes for an inhabitable world? For if we radically question the world in which the destruction of basic values is under way, if that world prompts the turn to a certain line of questioning, it is because of a fairly serious ethical disorientation. One reason we exclaim about the world in the way we do, acting as if this world was never included in any possible idea of the world we might have had, is that we are not sure how best to live in a world now organized around an unprecedented immunological crisis—we are not sure what a livable life would be in *this* world. And we see, perhaps more clearly than before—or in a different way—that the possibility of a livable life depends upon an inhabitable world. I wish to think about those two latter questions and see whether Scheler's formulation can help to answer them, or whether it meets its limits there.

To make a demand for a livable life is to demand that a given life has the power to live, to keep itself alive, and to wish for its life. If we ask the question *what makes a life livable?*, we do so precisely because we know that under some conditions it surely is not—for example, under unlivable conditions of poverty, incarceration, destitution, or social and sexual violence, including homophobic, transphobic, or racist violence and violence against women. Implicit in the question *how long can I live like this?* is an assumption that there must be other ways of living, and that we can—or, rather, must—distinguish between forms of life that are livable and those that are unlivable. When the question *how can I live like this?* converts into a conviction—"I will *not* continue to live like this"—we are in the midst of an urgent question both philosophical and social: What are the conditions that permit life to be lived in a way that affirms the continuation of life itself? And with whom shall I join my life in order to assert the values of our lives? These questions are different from *what is the good life?* or even the older existential question, *what is the meaning of life?*

As I suggested at the outset, the question of what makes a life livable is linked with the question *what makes for an inhabitable world?* This last was not Max Scheler's question, but it follows from the sense of the world that he describes, the world that he claims is exhibited through the tragic. When the world is an object immersed in sorrow, how is it possible to inhabit such a world? What about the persistence of uninhabitable sorrow? The answer lies less in individual conduct or practice than in the forms of solidarity that emerge, across whatever distance, to produce the conditions for inhabiting the world. Am I restoring the place of the subject to the discussion after Scheler has rather emphatically dismissed it? Or am I shifting the discussion to the question of life, of living, and the livable, and not just in the anthropocentric senses of those terms? We have considered the negative wonder, recoil, even shock: not the event as such but the world in which such an event can happen. But if such an event happens and the world proves to be a place where it can, then how to live in such a world? And how is such a world made livable?

This last question is slightly different from the second one I mentioned: *What is an* inhabitable *world?* This last question seems to overlap with *what does it mean to live a livable life?* But they remain two distinct questions. The first asserts the world as primary perhaps in the spirit of Scheler, but it adds the human back into the equation through its form of life, one that is connected to other life forms such that another question is spawned: how, then, can the world be inhabited by human and nonhuman creatures? The second asserts a distinction between a life that is livable and one that is unlivable, a distinction that actually belongs more properly to a spectrum of more and less livable lives.

When we ask about living in the world, we are already speaking about inhabiting the world, for there is no living without dwelling in the world. And dwelling brings up both duration and space. It would be different if we were speaking only about the earth. The earth persists in many places without being inhabited by humans, and that is a great relief amid climate destruction. The world, however, always implies a space and time of inhabitation. A world includes the temporal and spatial coordinates in which a life is lived—all the supports that provide for duration through space and time in relation to a network or field of living beings and built environments. If the world is *un*inhabitable, then destruction has had its way with the world. If a life is *un*livable, then the conditions of livability have been destroyed. The destruction of the earth through climate change makes for an uninhabitable world: it reminds us of the necessity to limit human inhabitation of the environment, for we cannot inhabit all of the earth without destroying the earth, and limits on where and how we live are necessary to preserve the earth, which in turn preserves our lives. Perhaps it sounds simplistic to say, but there are better and worse ways for humans to inhabit the world. And now the earth can survive—and regenerate—only if limits are set on the reach and disruption of human habitation. Humans impose limits on themselves to make for a habitable world under conditions of climate change. Parts of the world must remain uninhabitable for habitation to become possible. The world in which one lives includes the earth, depends upon the earth, cannot exist without the earth. Moreover, a life proves not to be livable if the world is not inhabitable. Part of what it means to live, then, and to live in a way that is livable, is to have a place to live, a part of the earth that can be inhabited without destroying it, to have shelter, and to be able to dwell as a body in a world that is sustained and safeguarded by the structures (and infrastructures) in which one lives—to be part of what is common, to share in a world in common.

To inhabit a world is part of what makes a life livable. So we cannot finally separate the question of an inhabitable world from a livable life. If we, as humans, inhabit the earth without regard for biodiversity, without stopping climate change, without limiting carbon emissions, then we produce for ourselves an uninhabitable world. The world may not be the same as the earth, but if we destroy the earth, we also destroy our worlds. And if we live human lives with no limits on our freedom, then we enjoy our freedom at the expense of a livable life. We make our own lives unlivable in the name of our freedom. Or, rather, we make our world uninhabitable and our lives unlivable in the name of a personal liberty and productivist imperative that are valued over all other values and become an instrument by which social bonds and livable worlds are destroyed. Personal liberty, in some of its variations, must be seen as world-destroying power. When personal liberty permits the destruction of others and the earth, then personal liberty claims destruction as its prerogative. I am certainly not against personal liberty, but the destructive form seems to me to be less about the person or the individual than about a nationalist sense of belonging and even a market sense of profit and gain that rationalizes the destruction of the earth and its climate. There is another form of freedom that is sidelined by this one, and it emerges amid social life, a life that seeks a common world, a life that is free to seek a common world.

This chapter has deliberately veered between philosophical investigation and political reflection in light of a present moment defined in part by the pandemic. I suggested earlier that there are some opposing views on what the pandemic prefigures about the social and economic world. We have seen that precarity and poverty have become intensified, and yet many are hopeful about redefining both sociality and solidarity during this time and are renewing demands for global, regional, and local networks of care and interdependency. The definitive boundaries of the body presumed by most forms of individualism have been called into question as the invariable porosity of the body—its openings, its mucosal linings, its windpipes—all become salient matters of life and death. How, then, do we rethink bodily relations of interdependency, intertwinement, and porosity during these times? Or, rather, how do these times and this world, already shifting in intensity, offer a chance to reflect upon interdependency, intertwinement, and porosity? Further, do these very concepts, notions, or ways of organizing sense experience give us a new way to understand social equality and inequality?

My wager is that the vexed and overlapping senses of sociality and livability can revise some of our key political concepts. If we did not know it before, it is now clear that the questioner is implicated in the question, and the question to some degree seeks to open up a thought, perhaps beyond the settled horizons of both academic inquiry and ordinary experience.

At the outset of this book, I note the distinction between the world and the planet, citing Mbembe, and suggest that the devastation of the planet requires a planetary strategy that would allow us to imagine a world, a common world in which to breathe. I also mentioned that Husserl set up a correlation between consciousness and its world, the noetic and noematic poles of intentionality, the structure of knowing experience. And I noted that Scheler sought in some ways to displace the transcendental subject with an emphasis on the world in its objectivity, understanding the tragic as a way in which the world leaves its impress and provokes a sorrow that exceeds the limits of experience, the horizon of the world. In this way, Scheler resonates with Wittgenstein, writing a few years later. With Maurice Merleau-Ponty, however, the entire idea of correlation proves impoverished in light of the embodied character of consciousness. The salient problem for him is neither that the world is structured in such a way that I may know it, nor that my modes of knowing are structured in such a way to adequately apprehend the world. Rather, it is that I am, as a body, part of the world I seek to know, already over there, seen, mobile, and mattering. The spatial limits of the perceived body belie its proper reach, for it is always both here and there, rooted and transported. The world that is usually assumed to be over there, or around me, is in fact already in and on me, and there is no easy way around that form of adherence, the way the world sticks to me and saturates me. My reflexivity, my very capacity to see or feel myself (if seeing is possible), oscillates between subject and object poles of experience. In "Eye and Mind," Merleau-Ponty puts it this way:

> My body simultaneously sees and is seen. That which looks at all things can also look at itself and recognize, in what it sees, the "other side" of its power of looking. It sees itself see-ing; it touches itself touching; it is visible and sensitive for itself. . . . It is a self [lacking transparency] through confu-sion, narcissism, through inherence of the one who sees in that which [one] sees, and through [the] inherence of sens-ing in the sensed—a self, therefore, that is caught up in things, that has a front and a back, a past and a future.

He continues, "things . . . are encrusted into its flesh, they are part of its full definition."[15]

In his posthumous work, *The Visible and the Invisible*, Merleau-Ponty goes even further. It is by virtue of a tangible world that I can touch anything at all. I could, I suppose, start to tell a story about when and how I first touched something, but the "I" who would narrate such a story postdates that first touch, that scene of touch/touching, by a long shot. This "I" is always catching up with the scene of touch that makes me possible, and no narrative reconstruction is possible, except perhaps through fiction and fantasy. The power of touch does not originate with me. The tangible understood as a field or a dimension of the world—a way in which the world is exhibited—is thus there as I touch something, and as I feel my own touch, or redouble my touch in touching something else. I touched that other person, but my own flesh gets in the way since at the moment of touch, I cannot evade my own touch in touching the other, although I may wish to. Indeed, the problem is not just that the dyadic scene of touch implies intertwinement. From the touch springs forth the tangible, understood as a field in which these cross-crossing object relations and self relations are condensed, constituted by this very reversibility and overlapping. So although my body is, for instance, over here (in pandemic conditions, it is too often over here, hemmed in, enclosed, or closed off) and is not elsewhere (except in those instances when it can be), it is still over there, in the objects I can or do touch precisely because this body belongs to a field of flesh (*le chair*), or a world of differentiated and overlapping flesh, whose instances are not exactly united but whose differences constitute the field itself. Flesh is the understanding of the delimited body from the point of view of dynamic interrelatedness.

Merleau-Ponty himself puts equal emphasis on the claim that "one cannot say that it is *here* or *now* in the sense that objects are." And although, he writes, "I am always on the same side of my body," what I touch opens up a world of objects and surfaces that are touched and touchable by others.[16] Even though I am not joined with that unity or those others who have touched that same surface, or are touching it now, or will surely touch it in the future, those disparate moments nevertheless imply one another, are linked with one another, although they are never summarized in a temporal or conceptual unity in any one person's mind. Echoing Scheler's contention that the tragic illuminates or discloses something constitutive about the world, Merleau-Ponty insists that the act discloses its condition of possibility: in naming, the name-able is opened up; in seeing, the visible looms; and in touching, the tangible leaves its impress upon us.

Merleau-Ponty here rewrites intersubjectively as intertwinement [*entrelac*], which implies interconnection, and interrelatedness, in which a fine distinction is not always possible to draw between the elements that impinge upon each other: the touch of the other is something that I feel, and in some sense, I touch what is touching me in the act of being touched. In this way, every passivity fails to become absolute. And if I imagine myself as only doing the touching, the only doer in the scene, my pretensions are undone because there is always this receptivity of the other's flesh—a being touched in the very act of touching. Receptivity is already a touching back. The polarities of activity and passivity are complicated in this view, as is the distinct way of separating consciousness from its world. The body and its senses introduce a sense of bodies interlaced with one another that moves beyond such binary oppositions. The ways we are bound up with one another are not precisely contingent. To be a body at all is to be bound up with others and with objects, with surfaces, and the elements, including the air that is breathed in and out, air that belongs to no one and everyone.

I suggest that this way of thinking has both ethical and political consequences for our times, for it offers a way of understanding interdependency that moves beyond the ontology of isolated individuals encased in discrete bodies. Perhaps this is what we already know pre-philosophically, but perhaps as well phenomenology can articulate this nascent or emergent understanding for our times. This conception of lives intertwined and interdependent has to be brought into a broader political understanding of climate change as well. A way forward for phenomenology might link the idea of an inhabitable world to the condition of climate destruction. If life depends on air that is passed among us, and on food and shelter derived from the resources of nature and labor, then climate destruction brings these life requirements to the fore in a different way than does the pandemic.

Air, water, shelter, clothing, and access to health care are not only sites of anxiety within the pandemic and compromised under climate change, but they also constitute requirements of life, of continuing to live, and it is the poor who suffer most from not having clean water, proper shelter, breathable air, access to health care. So under conditions of deprivation, the question of whether one is living a livable life is an urgent economic one: are there health service and shelters and clean enough water for any number of people to live, and for all those who are related to me to live? The existential urgency of the question is heightened by economic precarity, and that precarity is intensified under the present conditions of pandemic.

Of course, humans have different experiences of the limit of livability. And whether a set of restrictions are livable depends on how one gauges the requirements of one's life. "Livability" is ultimately a modest requirement. One is not, for instance, asking *what will make me happy?* Nor is one asking *what kind of life would most clearly satisfy my desires?* One is looking, rather, to live in such a way that life itself remains bearable so that one can continue to live. In other words, one is looking for those requirements of a life that allow a life to be sustained and to persist. Another way of saying this would be *what are the conditions of life that make possible the desire to live?* For we surely know that under some conditions of restriction—incarceration, occupation, detention, torture, statelessness—one may ask *is life worth living under these conditions?* And in some cases, the very desire to live is extinguished, and people do take their lives, or submit to slower forms of death dealt by slower forms of violence.

The pandemic poses questions that are specifically ethical, for the restrictions under which I am asked to live are those that protect not just my own life but the lives of others as well. Our lives are knotted together or, perhaps, intertwined. The restrictions stop me from acting in certain ways, but they also lay out a vision of the interconnected world that I am asked to accept. If they were to speak, they would ask me to understand this life that I live as bound up with other lives and to regard this "being bound up with one another" as a fundamental feature of who I am. I am not fully sealed as a bounded creature but emit breath into a shared world where I take in air that has been circulating through the lungs of others. The reason I am restricted from visiting any number of places is both self-protection and the protection of others: I am being stopped from contracting a virus that could take my life but also from communicating a virus that I may not know that I have and that could debilitate or take the lives of others. In other words, I am asked not to die and not to put others at risk of illness or death. The same kinds of actions bear the same sorts of risks. So I must decide whether to comply with that request. To understand and accept both parts of that request, I must understand myself as capable of communicating the virus but also as someone who can be infected by the virus, so potentially both acting and acted upon. There is no escape from either end of that polarity, a risk that correlates with the twofold dimension of breathing itself: inhalation, exhalation. It seems as if I am bound up with others through the prospect of doing or suffering harm in relation to them. The ethical quandary, or vector, that the pandemic produces begins with the insight that my life and the lives of others depend upon a recognition of how our lives depend in part upon how each of us acts. So my action holds your life, and your action holds mine, at least potentially. If I come from a state like the United States, where self-interest governs everyday moral deliberations, and if I am a privileged citizen within such a state, I am used to acting on my own behalf and deciding whether and how a consideration of others comes into play. But in the ethical paradigm that belongs to the pandemic, I am already in relation to you, and you are already in relation to me way before either of us starts to deliberate on how best to relate to one another. We are quite literally in each other's bodies without any deliberate intention to be there. If we were not, we would have no fear. We share air and surfaces, we brush up against each other by accident or by design or consent; we are strangers near each other on the plane, and the package I wrap may be the one you open or carry or drop at my door at the moment when I open the door and we find ourselves face to face. According to prevailing frameworks of self-interest, we act as if our separate lives come first and then we decide on our social arrangements—this is a liberal conceit that underwrites a great deal of moral philosophy. We somehow exist before and outside the contracts that bind us, and we give up our individuality and unrestrained freedom when we enter those contracts. But why do we assume individuality from the start when it is clearly formed and, as psychoanalysis contends, a tenuous achievement at best? If we ask *how and when did my life first become imaginable as a separate life?*, we can see that the question itself starts to unfold an answer. Individuality is an imagined status and depends on specifically social forms of the imaginary. In fact, the early stages of infancy are marked by primary helplessness, and the survival of the infant depends on a range of materials and practices of care that secure nutrition, shelter, and warmth. The question of food and sleep and shelter were never separable from the question of one's life, its very livability. Those provisions must have been there, even if minimally, for any of us to begin a life that would come to include the imagining of a separate "I." That dependency on others, on provisions, on all that we could not possibly give ourselves, had to be put aside if not fully denied for any of us to decide one day that one is a singular individual, distinct and spatially closed off from others, not only separated but *separate*.

All individuation is haunted by a dependency that is imagined as if it could be overcome or has already been vanquished. And yet individuals fully isolated and on their own in the pandemic are among the most imperiled. How to live without touch or being touched, without the shared breath? Is that livable? If my "life" is from the start only ambiguously my own, then the field of social interdependency enters from the start, prior to any deliberation on moral conduct or the benefits of social contracts voluntarily entered (not all are voluntary). The question *what should I do?* or even *how do I live this life?* presupposes an "I" and a "life" that poses that question on its own and for itself alone. But if we accept that the "I" is always populated and life is always implicated in other lives and life forms, then how do those moral questions change? How have they already changed under conditions of pandemic?

Of course, it is difficult to shake the presumption that when we talk about this life, we are talking about this discrete and bounded individual life and its finitude. No one can die in my place. No one can even go to the bathroom in my place! Further, what makes a life livable seems to be a personal question pertaining to this life and not to any other life. And yet when I ask what makes "a life" livable, I seem to accept that some shared conditions make human lives livable. If so, then at least some part of what makes my own life livable makes another life livable as well, and I cannot then fully dissociate the question of my own well-being from the well-being of others. The virus does not let us think another way—unless, of course, we turn away from what we know about the virus, as some notorious government officials have done, dragging countless others along with them. If the pandemic gives us one rather large social and ethical lesson to learn, my wager is that this seems to be it: What makes a life livable is a question that implicitly shows us that the life we live is never exclusively our own, that the conditions for a livable life have to be secured, and not just for me but for lives and living processes more generally. Those conditions cannot be grasped, for instance, if the category of private property that describes my body or that presumes my individuality is accepted as a methodology. The "I" who I am is also to some extent a "we" even as tensions tend to mark the relation of these two senses of one's life. If it is this life that is mine, it seems then to be mine alone, and the logic of identity has won the argument with a tautological flourish. But if my life is never fully my own, if life names a condition and trajectory that is shared, then life is the place where I lose my self-centeredness and discover the porous character of my embodiment. In fact, the phrase "my life" tends to pull in two directions at once: this life, singular, irreplaceable; this life, shared and human, shared as well with animal lives and with various systems and networks of life. I require living processes and living others to live, which means that I am nothing without them. This life, I would suggest, is densely populated before I start to live it and must be for me to live at all. Others precede me, anticipate me to some degree, and their provisioning and early effects— loving impingements, as it were—start to form this person who eventually comes to refer to itself as "I." So the "I" never comes into being except through the support and company of others, through living processes, and through the social institutions on which the living human creature depends and to which it is necessarily connected. The desires and actions of those others—their ways of handling or neglecting me—set me in motion and give me form, imprinting and establishing me as one with desires and capable of action, creating a worldly connection, bringing joy and pain, suffering loss, seeking repair. I cannot come into being without being touched, handled, and maintained, and I cannot touch or handle or maintain without having first been formed in the crucible of those practices. And yet when the conditions of touch are lost, so too is a fundamental sense of what sustains us as living creatures whose capacities for receiving and doing are layered together over time.

Because certain conditions of life and living are laid bare by the circulation of the virus, we now have a chance to grasp our relations to the earth and to each other in sustaining ways, to understand ourselves less as separated entities driven by self-interest than as complexly bound together in a living world that requires our collective resolve to struggle against its destruction, the destruction of what bears incalculable value—the ultimate sense of the tragic.

Chapter 2

POWERS IN THE PANDEMIC

REFLECTIONS ON RESTRICTED LIFE

HOW, THEN, do we rethink bodily relations of interdependency, intertwinement, and porosity during these times? And is there a way to revisit what we mean by social equality and inequality in the context of bodily interdependency? What difference would it make to rethink equality in light of bodily interdependency? Taking the destruction of the environment and systemic racism into account, we are compelled to ask whether we can illuminate how the vexed and overlapping senses of sociality and livability can revise some of our key political concepts.

I referred briefly to the distinction between the world and the planet, citing Mbembe, suggesting that the devastation of the planet requires a planetary strategy that would allow us to imagine a common world in which to breathe. The relation between the pandemic and climate change has been brought into focus. Some have argued that climate change makes pandemics more possible, and others have suggested that we can learn some lessons from the pandemic for opposing climate destruction.[1]

CLIMATES OF LIFE AND WORK

Without entering into the debate over whether the pandemic is a direct or indirect effect of climate change, I believe it is imperative to situate the pandemic global condition in the midst of climate change, for both foreground a sense of global interdependency as a life-or-death matter. Whatever sense of world we bring to this discussion is at least partially inflected by this question of continuing environmental destruction. That means we are living in a pandemic in the midst of environmental racism and within its terms, exemplified by unsafe water in poor regions and increasing numbers of evictions for many with uncertain income. The relation to air, water, shelter, and food—already compromised under the conditions of climate change and unbridled capitalism—are even more acutely registered under pandemic conditions. These are two different conditions, but they become linked together and intensified in the present. Those structures did not disappear; they intensified. On the one hand, the cessation of travel and economic activity allows the sea and air to recover from protracted contamination by environmental toxins. On the other hand, we only glimpsed what environmental renewal or repair might be before production ramped up again. Still, the pandemic has illuminated how the natural world could regenerate if production were cut back, if travel were curtailed, and if carbon emissions and footprints were diminished or eradicated.

I would like, ideally, to link the interconnected character of our lives to the obligation we have to organize the world, including health care, on principles of radical equality. The question of whether to open the economy that is posed from the perspective of lockdown and "restart the world" in regions where confinement has been instituted for protracted periods of time assumes that restarting the economy will not lead to illness and death for many people. In the spring of 2022, some governments, most notably Boris Johnson's, declared the pandemic over or insisted that all precautions could be thrown to the wind. And yet such decisions establish a dispensable population who must now take it upon themselves to isolate or risk their lives. These include those with autoimmune conditions, diabetes, lung conditions, and all those who, because of age or access to vaccines, lack sufficient antibodies. The decision to refuse masking and episodic confinement altogether as an approach assumes that some people will fall ill and die, but, the argument goes, that is a small price to pay in order to keep the economy open and flourishing. Keeping the economy open is, of course, important, especially for those who are poor or who risk falling into poverty and debt without employment. But what are the risks for them? Indeed, many workers have faced a question: do I continue to work in order to "make a living" even if "making a living" makes me die? It is not a question of work or death but death *as a result of* work, even when work is precisely what one needs to live. The contradiction is one that Marx pointed out long ago, but for him the condition was capitalism, not the pandemic (although for much of his writing life, a pandemic was there in the background). Under capitalism, the worker works in order to secure a wage that allows the worker and the worker's family to secure subsistence. And yet by working under conditions that do not protect the health of the worker, the worker risks their life. And by working hours that wear down the body, the worker suffers injury and illness and becomes decapacitated as a worker. By working under such conditions, in other words, the worker ceases to be able to work and can no longer provide subsistence for themselves and their family or dependents. This means that by working, the worker comes close to death or dies, rather than securing the conditions for a livable life. The contradiction, according to Marx, could only be resolved through the dissolution of capitalism; in our present moment, the contradiction can only be resolved by a guaranteed annual income and a reanimation of socialist ideals. Indeed, if income were secure, no worker would have to face the situation of having to work under perilous conditions in order to live. Living with that anxiety is not a livable life. This is not an equitable or life-supporting organization of common life.

The pandemic takes place both in the context of climate change and environmental destruction and, for the most part, within the terms of a capitalism that continues to treat the lives of workers as dispensable. Times have changed since Marx wrote his description of the life-and-death struggle of the worker. For some of us, there is now health insurance and safety measures in the workplace, along with other provisions of social welfare. But for the vast majority of people, there is no health insurance, and the effort to secure health care is a struggle that too often fails.

So, when we ask in the United States, for instance, whose lives are most imperiled by the pandemic, we find that it is the poor, the Black community, the recent migrants, the incarcerated, the immunocompromised, and the elderly. As businesses reopen and industry restarts—or opens and closes in quick succession—there is no way to protect so many workers from the virus. And for populations that never had access to health care or who were disadvantaged by racism, illnesses that once could have been treated become "preexisting conditions," making those people more vulnerable to the illness and to death. By the summer of 2021, at least, several countries had seen zero vaccines, the majority of them in Africa. These global inequalities are reflected in the woefully low vaccination rates in 2022 in Burundi, Tanzania, the Democratic Republic of the Congo, and Haiti.

Those who believe that "the health of the economy" is more important than the "health of the population" adhere to the belief that profit and wealth are finally more important than human life. Those who are calculating the risks, who know that some people will have to die, conclude either implicitly or explicitly that human life will be sacrificed for the economy. Throughout the pandemic some people have argued that industry and workplaces should stay open for the sake of the working poor. But if it is precisely the working poor whose lives will be sacrificed at the workplace, where the infection rates are highest, then we are returned to that fundamental contradiction Marx laid out nearly two hundred years ago.[2] We open the economy—or keep it open—in order to sustain the lives of the working poor, but the working poor are those whose lives are deemed dispensable by opening the economy, whose work can be replaced by other workers, whose lives do not count as singular and invaluable lives. In other words, under the conditions of pandemic, the worker goes to work in order to live, but work is precisely what hastens the worker's death. The worker discovers her dispensability and replaceability. According to that logic, the health of the economy is more important than the health of the worker. So the old contradiction that belongs to capitalism assumes a new form under pandemic conditions.

As policymakers in 2021–22 reckoned on the costs of reopening the economy, they understood that many people would die, that those who would be disproportionately exposed to illness and death were precisely those who were not only without adequate health care but also had no choice but to work. Or they are those who are incarcerated or detained at the border—they do not have the power to move or even to move away from others. Social distance is a privilege, and not everyone can establish those spatial conditions. In shelters where many people live in proximity, the conditions for securing one's own health simply do not exist. The structural forms of racism become explicit as Black and brown people in the United States, and the poor everywhere, become the most likely to succumb. We see a calculation at work: how many lives are worth losing? Whose lives are worth losing? Whose lives were never considered lives worth safeguarding to begin with?

Some of these same questions have been at the center of the Movement for Black Lives at the very moment when many Black and brown communities have been suffering the loss or absence of decent health care. The murder of George Floyd, along with a long and lengthening list of names of Black people murdered by police in the United States, has shifted and intensified an already pervasive sense of peril—not only because yet another Black life was extinguished by brutal police force but also because the spectacle of his killing was a shameless advertisement for white supremacy, a resurgence of lynching explicitly performed for the cell phone video. It is still the neck, once again the chokehold. The collective trauma for Black people cannot be underestimated in its intergenerational and present form, especially now, when so many Black lives are claimed by Covid-19 because health care is inadequate, inaccessible, or unaffordable. The disproportionate number of deaths in communities of color more generally speaks to a systemic racism within a broken and brutal health care system. The very same community that mourns the loss of lives that could have, and should have, been treated and saved, suffers at the same time the police violence against Black bodies on the street. If Michel Foucault thought there was a difference between taking another's life and letting another die, we see that police violence that takes life works in tandem with health systems that let death happen. It is systemic racism that links the two.

I am not convinced that these are competing crises or dueling disasters. They are linked together. The systemic racism that we find instanced in the health care system that fails Black and brown communities follows from the failure to institute health care as a basic public good to which every person should be able to lay claim. The demand that Black and brown people work for a service economy that allows others with money to stay home and away from stores follows from a system that demands that everyone work for a wage even if the conditions of work are hazardous—when it should be countered by a guaranteed national income that would make sure no worker has to make that choice between economic destitution and serious illness.

Perhaps we were wrong to think, even for a brief duration, that the pandemic could function as a great leveler, that it would be the occasion for imagining a more substantial equality and a more radical form of justice. We were not exactly wrong, but neither were we well prepared to bring about the world we imagined. One problem is that the aspiration animating the idea of remaking the world presumed it as a tabula rasa, a new beginning, without asking whether the new brings a weighty history along with it, whether new beginnings are really breaks with the past, or even can be. Another problem, clearly deeper, is that the economy very quickly came to replace the world in the mainstream public discourse. The "health of the economy" was understood to be more valuable and urgent than the "health of the people." Indeed, attributing health to the economy figured the economy as a human body, an organism, one whose life and growth must be supported at all costs, even if that entails the loss of human life. But the transposition of health onto the economy did not just transfer a human attribute to the markets; it literally drained health from living bodies to establish health for the economy. That has been a deadly form of displacement and inversion within the logic of capitalism that comes to the fore within pandemic times.

If the anthropomorphized health of the economy comes at the expense of the health of those who are workers, minorities, the poor, those with already compromised health, then the figure of economic "health" does not merely borrow the "life" of those bodies as it represents the economy as a form of organic life. It takes that life; it drains that life; it expresses the willingness to sacrifice those lives. And in those senses it is a life-taking figuration. The false consolation of the cost–benefit model of economic calculation is that it allows for the health and life of the body to be replaced by a number, a percentage, and a graphic curve. The latter, however, is not a simple representation of the living body but, in this context at least, becomes the means of its effacement. The graphic sign and number is meant to show us how many or how few have died, and if the curve is flattening, we are supposed to rejoice because only so many people are dying now, and that is apparently great news. Presently, it has provided the alibi to reopen the market economy and re-spike the virus and its newer variants; in that way, the graphic curve imperils the lives and deaths it purports to represent. The point of the curve is precisely to establish the level of illness and death that we can accept as reasonable, the right number of deaths, the right extension of the horizontal line, the level that establishes the number of deaths we are willing to live with in order to keep markets open. As a representational form, the graph sanitizes those deaths, or allegorizes its general sanitization, another borrowing from the metaphorics of health in the service of a necropolitical plan—exemplifying perhaps in a remarkably vivid way the death drive thriving at the heart of the capitalist machine. But that is another project.

No worries: I am not claiming that the living body does not require representation. I am not even claiming we have no need for graphs. We certainly do have those needs. Bodily life actually depends upon representations that make clear what are the requirements of living. Yet the question remains: which representations will do? I am not saying that figures kill, but they do exhibit the trajectory of a violence that depends upon a sanitizing disavowal for its reproduction. If the world were replaced with the economy, and the economy (understood as a market economy and a financial market) were understood as undergoing a health crisis, then it would become our responsibility to go back to work, to reopen the economy for business, to flood the churches and the gyms, even if that clearly meant that the virus would spread and more people would lose their health, even their lives. Unspoken here is the terrifying presumption that working lives are dispensable as are the lives of all those who are unsheltered or whose sheltering does not take place in a bourgeois household with closed doors and property lines. Unspoken here is the dispensability of all those lives thinking they are embracing freedom as they head toward illness and death, their own or that of others they may not know. Is it possible, then, to reclaim the world from the economy? To disarticulate the rebooting of the market from the making of a world—that would be the first step toward a promising remaking of the world.

And we have come to see more clearly, and through a different lens, that a radical inequality among living beings was always part of what phenomenology has called "the lifeworld."

Some lives have to be protected against death at all costs. And safeguarding other lives is considered not worth it—not worth the cost.

FUTURES OF THE LIFEWORLD

With the idea of the lifeworld we have a chance to bring together our two questions: What makes a life livable? And what constitutes an inhabitable world? Under provisional confinement, we may have felt, or continue to feel, that the lack of contact, physical touch, and social gathering has been unbearable, and yet we do bear these losses in order to protect lives. Sheltering in place is not prison. We accept confinement not only to protect ourselves but because we are aware of our capacity to infect others. We live, as it were, in an ethical vector in which we can be infected or infecting, a situation that establishes us as beings who are constantly shedding parts of ourselves in the direction of others, who are receiving fragments of others as a matter of course.

At the beginning of the pandemic, when we did not understand that its transmission was through the air, we feared the surfaces of the world. And we may well have become aware that we share the surfaces of the world, the handles we touch, the packages we open. We are everywhere in each other's hands, which means that the very condition of our sociality becomes lethal under pandemic conditions. Yes, parts of the suspended world still break in under confinement—words of love and support, art, community, and laughter over the wires or through the internet. Such connections can be both virtual and visceral and should not be underestimated as life sustaining. But this ethical vector that we are raises broader questions about how partially unknowing we are about how we are affecting others or how others might be affecting us. Our ethical obligations are afflicted with opacity. What seems clear is that we can no longer act only in self-interest since this embodied self is situated socially, already outside itself in the environment and others, affected and affecting. My interest turns out to be your interest since the life that is mine is also bound up with yours, as yours is with mine. And this is true not only under pandemic conditions but in the interdependent social world in which our lives take form and make sense. For the fact is that we share the surfaces and objects of the world, and traces of others we do not know pass between us, sometimes unknowingly. What you touch thus touches me, although not always. If I touch a surface, am I also potentially touching another or being touched by them? It is unclear whether you are affecting me or I am affecting you, and perhaps neither one of us can know at the time whether that affecting/affected is also a form of infecting/infected. When we think about the relationship of bodies to one another, we are not simply talking about discrete entities that exist in isolation from one another. But neither are we talking about a simple reciprocity. There is earth and air and food that mediates our relationship, and we belong to those regions as much as we belong to one another.

As I noted earlier, Merleau-Ponty's posthumously published reflections on tactility rely upon the figure of the "*entrelac*"— the interlacing.[3] He tells us that when we touch an object, we become aware of ourselves touching as well, and that the tangible world, everything in the world we touch, is always defined in part by the fact that it is touchable by us. At the same time, the tangible world exceeds our touch and establishes the general conditions of tactility. And that excess makes itself known in the touch itself. In this way we cannot conceive of ourselves as beings capable of touch without the tangible objects of the world. And when we near and touch one another, do we always know at that moment who precisely is touching whom? When we say "we touched each other," and we seem to be reporting on an emotional or physical encounter. If my hand touches another, it is at the very same time touched by that other bodily surface, animate and animating. That means that the other also touches me, whether or not I think of myself as receptive. Of course, receptivity is not the same as passivity, and yet the two are all too often conflated. Further, if activity and passivity are intertwined, as Merleau-Ponty suggests, then both action and receptivity have to be thought outside the logic of mutual exclusion. Following Spinoza, the greater the potentials of receptivity, the greater the powers of action.[4]

This notion of intertwining compels a reformulation of basic questions: Am I subject or object or always both, and what difference does it make to understand one's body as bound to a tangible world? If, as Merleau-Ponty points out, touching another is also the experience of touching oneself or becoming aware of one's own skin at the point of contact, is there a way to distinguish between this scene of touching / being touched and a sense of the tactility of the self? Is there, in other words, an equivocation between acting and receiving that marks an embodied and tactile sense of self? There are moments of touch in which one poses questions about oneself: Who am I at this moment of touch, or who am I becoming? Or to follow the question posed by María Lugones, who have I become by virtue of this new tactile encounter with another?[5] Any teenager in the course of coming out finds this existential/social quandary emerging precisely then and there, in a proximity and intimacy whose form one could not have fully anticipated. This is how tactility works, Merleau-Ponty tells us, insofar as the porous boundaries of the body mark out paths of relationality; affected by that which we seek to affect, there is no clear way to distinguish activity and passivity as mutually exclusive. Aristotle bites the dust again.

Why bring Scheler and Merleau-Ponty together in the way that I have? Is the destruction of value that defines the tragic for Scheler really something that speaks to us now? Is the notion of the world indicted or laid bare by the tragic event something that we can now bring forward as we seek to understand the coordinates of the world in which we are now asked to live? Is this world inhabitable? If so, for whom? And in what measure? What happens when the destruction of value—such as the value of lives, the values of the earth—drenches the world in sorrow? What happens when we lose touch or can barely remember the proximate breath of another? Who are we then or, rather, what world is it that we then inhabit, if inhabitation is in fact still possible? Perhaps the disorientations of a subject-centered view of the world carries with it signs of hope or promise of another kind of world-making, another way of living in the world of air and earth, architectural enclosures, narrow passageways, as a breathing and tactile creature who requires so many human and nonhuman dimensions of life to live.

Merleau-Ponty thought that the human body was dispersed in time and space in the way that other objects and things were not. What he did not consider, however, was that objects and things carry with them natural histories, to use Theodor Adorno's phrase, the history of work and consumption, and a mediation by market values.[6] This is especially true when we think about extractivism as the plundering of natural resources for the purposes of profit. If the intersubjective relation is formulated without reference to the object world—that is, to the environment, to the complex values of natural goods, and to the broader organization of economic and social reality—then it is no longer possible to understand both the values it produces and those it destroys. If a notion of the inhabitable world fails to include the effects of environmental toxins on breathable air, then what is lost is the very idea of the climate as part of the horizon of the world. Further, without those references, we cannot know how to live well and how best to inhabit the earth or to make an inhabitable world. Living in a livable way requires inhabiting a world—a world that remains inhabitable. Objects can be vectors for all these questions, perhaps more clearly than an exclusive focus on subjectivity or its variant, intersubjectivity. For Merleau-Ponty, the dyadic relation between you and me is both conditioned and exceeded by tangibility itself, by language, but also, we might add, by breathability—the social character of air.

Even though science has minimized the chances of transmission by objects, we might have to look more carefully at the object world to understand its relation to heightened conditions of transmissibility. After all, as a social form, the object is constituted by a set of social relationships. It is made, consumed, and distributed within socioeconomic organizations of life. This general truth takes on a new significance under the conditions of pandemic: why is the person who drops off food still working even though it may expose her to the virus more readily than someone who receives food from a courier? The dire character of this question is, of course, intensified for those who are unvaccinated, whether by choice or because vaccines are inaccessible or unaffordable, or because one's autoimmunity is such that vaccines fail to protect. Too often the choice workers have faced is to risk illness and possible death or to lose one's job. A virus never belongs to any one body that contracts it. It is neither a possession nor an attribute, even though we say "so and so *has* the virus." The model of property cannot provide a way of understanding the virus. Rather, the virus seems *to have* that person: it comes from elsewhere, takes that person into its grip, transfers onto a mucosal surface or into an orifice through touch or breath, takes the body as its host, burrowing there, entering cells and directing their replication, spreading its tendrils, only to be released into the air and potentially enter other living creatures. The virus lands on, enters a body partially defined by its porosity, and departs to land on another body, looking for a host—the skin, the nostril, the aperture. Under the most severe versions of lockdown, people seemed to fear close contact, the aerial relay of the virus from face to face. The face-to-face encounter is surely now (under Omicron or Delticron, as of this writing) more widely feared than any contamination through the handled object (although research on surfaces or fomites continues to surprise), and it now appears that the aerosol relay is the clearly preponderant form of viral transfer.[7] Rarely do we have full control over our proximity to others in the daily course of life: the social world is unpredictable that way. Unwilled proximity to objects and others is a feature of public life and seems normal for anyone who takes public transit or needs to move along a street in a densely populated city: we bump into each other in narrow spaces, we lean on the railing or toward another person when we speak, we touch whatever is in our way, often getting close to strangers with whom transactions are required or who simply live and move in the shared spaces of the world. And yet that condition of chance contact and encounter, of brushing up against one another, becomes potentially fatal when that contact increases the potential of illness and that illness carries the risk of death. Under these conditions, the objects and others we require appear as potentially the greatest threats to our lives. This continuing paradox has been, as one knows, barely livable.

In the pandemic, however, we found ourselves asking whether we wanted to live in this world structured by distance and isolation, by no or limited work, and by fear of debt and death, and whether such a world is inhabitable. Yes, we found ways to keep company and community in the worst surges of the virus, to put art into the world, to keep visceral connections alive through virtual means, virtual connections alive through visceral means. But the problem of radical inequality haunts every phase of pandemic time: whose lives are considered valuable as lives and whose are not? What may appear abstract philosophical questions turn out to be those that emerge from the heart of a social and epidemiological emergency or, indeed, a crisis. For the world to be inhabitable, it must support the conditions of life as well as the desire to live. For who wants to live in a world that so easily dispenses with one's life, or the lives of one's friends or family, or with entire populations with whom one cohabits the earth? To want to live in such a world is to take up the struggle against the very powers that all too easily dispose of lives, life-forms, and living habitats. One cannot oppose all that brutality alone but only through collaboration, expanding networks of support that make provisions for new conditions for living and reconfigured space-times for desire, enacting a new form of common life and collective values and desires. And for a life to be livable, it has to be embodied—that is, it requires whatever supports allow for a space to be inhabited—and it needs a space, a shelter or dwelling, to live. Housing and accessible infrastructure are thus essential preconditions of a livable life. But those spaces are not restricted to house and home; they include the workplace, the store, the street, the field, the village, the metropole, the means of transport, the public and protected lands, and the public square.

As vaccines are increasingly available in countries that can pay or that have the capacity to produce unpatented vaccines, the financial markets have predictably started to invest in the futures of this or that pharmacological industry (antivirals like Paxlovid will surely make a difference if they are widely distributed and made accessible). The radical inequality that characterizes the global distribution of vaccines reminds us that the effort to bring the pandemic to an end must be linked to the struggle to overcome profound global inequalities. We must struggle for a world in which we defend the rights to health care for the stranger on the far side of the world as fervently as we do for our neighbor or lover. That may seem unreasonably altruistic, but perhaps it is now time to take apart the local and nationalist bias that pervades our idea of the reasonable. In 2020 the World Health Organization director, Tedros Adhanom Ghebreyesus, formulated an ethical precept that took "the world" to be its measure, suggesting that such a concept may be central to ethical reflection going forward: "None of us can accept a world in which some people are protected while others are not."[8] He was calling for an end to nationalism and to the market rationality that would calculate which lives are more worth safeguarding and saving than others by indexing borders and profit. But he was also telling us that the virus will continue to circulate as long as some people remain infected/infectious: no one is safe until everyone is safe. This relatively simple epidemiological truth thus coincides with an ethical imperative. From both perspectives, then, it follows that a commitment to global forms of collaboration and support that seek to ensure equal access to health care, to a livable life. To do that we have to be mindful of the potentials released by the question *what kind of world is this?* and to derive from the one question another: *in what kind of world do we wish to live?* I have not answered the question of what makes a life livable or a world inhabitable. But I do hope that I am helping to keep such questions open and debatable. My own sense, however, is that the lifeworlds in which we live have to be those that secure the conditions of life for all creatures whose persistence and desire to live should be equally honored. As epidemiologists counsel us that making Covid-19 endemic is the way to solve the current problem, we have to ask whether there is, even then, an assumption at work that some part of the world population will have to lose their lives. They never gained access to vaccines, or they never were persuaded by the argument that vaccines would help them, or they belong to the immunocompromised for whom vaccines are not working. To refuse to accept a solution in which some have to die so that most can live is to refuse a crass utilitarianism in favor of a more radical equality for the living. It implies confronting critically the market-driven calculation that would force us to make such choices.

Only a global commitment can honor global interdependency. To undertake such a task, we have to renew and revise our understanding of what we mean by *a world*, an inhabitable world, one understood as a way of already and always being implicated in each other's life. At the height of pandemics, that interdependency can sometimes seem fatal, pushing us back into notions of protective individuality and domestic "safety" (Was that ever safe for women? For queer kids?). And yet interdependency is also the way out. It implies a vision of global health, equal accessibility, free vaccines, and the end to profit-mongering by pharmaceuticals. Interdependency is also the possibility we may have for sensual ecstasy, for the support we need to live, and for radical equality and alliances committed to building and sustaining a livable world in common. We can fall back into our personal lives if we have economic resources, wonder when the world will open more so that we can resume our activities and relations, or become ever more despondent about the thwarting of our self-interest. But this most personal isolation and frustration is one that is shared across the world. Some manically oppose vaccines only to see the virus taking their own lives or the lives of those they love. We also see the hypernationalist response that makes use of the pandemic to consolidate state powers in authoritarian forms, strengthening borders and the use of surveillance technology, engaging in xenophobia, and shoring up the heteronormative domestic sphere. But for those who are still striving for a common world amid lethal inequalities and geopolitical forms of domination, it is a vexed situation as we cling to the scattered and oscillating moments of promise as the pandemic is proclaimed over right before the new surge.

However differently we register this pandemic, we understand it as global; it brings home the fact that we are implicated in a shared world. Some may rail against the global pandemic, shoring up nationalism, but the frantic character of their efforts concede the very global nature of pandemic relationality. The capacity of living human creatures to affect one another has always been a matter of life or death, but only under some historical conditions does this become most clear to see. Of course, this is not exactly *a common world* we share, and to recognize the pandemic as global means confronting those inequalities. The pandemic has illuminated and intensified racial and economic inequalities at the same time that it heightens the global sense of what our obligations are to one another and the earth. There is movement in a global direction, one based on a new sense of mortality and interdependency, the result of stark realities of climate destruction and pandemic. The experience of finitude is coupled with a keen sense of inequality: who dies early and why, and for whom is there no infrastructural or social promise of life's continuity?

This sense of the interdependency of the world, strengthened by a common immunological predicament, challenges our notion of ourselves as isolated individuals encased in discrete bodies, bound by established borders. Who now could deny that to be a body at all is to be bound up with other living creatures, with surfaces, and the elements, including the air that belongs to no one and everyone, that all remind us of the life that can only persist beyond—and against—property relations?

Within these pandemic times, air, water, shelter, clothing, and access to health care are sites of individual and collective anxiety. All these life requirements were already imperiled by climate change. Whether or not one is living a livable life is not only a private existential question but an urgent economic one, incited by the life-and-death consequences of social inequality: are there health services and shelters and clean enough water for all those who should have an equal share of this world? The question is made more urgent by conditions of heightened economic precarity during the pandemic, exposing the ongoing climate catastrophe as well for the threat to livable life that it is.

An inhabitable world for humans depends on a flourishing earth that does not have humans at its center. We oppose environmental toxins not only so humans can live and breathe without fear of being poisoned but also because the water and the air must have lives that are not centered on our own or in our service. As we dismantle the rigid forms of individuality in these interconnected times, we can imagine the smaller part that human worlds must play on this earth whose regeneration we depend upon—and which, in turn, depends upon our diminished and more mindful role.[9] An inhabitable earth requires that we do not inhabit all of the earth, that we not only limit the reach of human habitation and production but also come to know and heed what the earth requires.

Chapter 3

INTERTWINING AS ETHICS AND POLITICS

IN THE last two chapters I have invoked some texts from the phenomenological tradition to illuminate some aspects of the pandemic that bear on sociality, interdependency, and embodiment. In doing so, I do not mean to claim that phenomenology is the only useful framework or that one can derive all significant claims about our times from that framework. I draw from phenomenology when and where it seems useful, and I put some aspects of phenomenology into conversation with other theoretical commitments, including Marx, anti-racist critique and—as will become increasingly clear—feminist and queer theory.

Husserl's own reflections on the practice of "bracketing" came under criticism by both Sartre and Merleau-Ponty.[1] They insisted that one did not need a deliberate method to suspend our everyday assumptions about the world in order to make the world into a matter of phenomenological analysis. There were historical experiences in which the constituted structure of the world was suddenly called into question or exhibited. These are moments of being exposed in one's naivete, perhaps humiliating or exhilarating. When Max Scheler, writing contemporaneously with Husserl, argued that the tragic indicated that something of value has been destroyed and that, on the occasion of that destruction, something about the constitution of the world is exhibited, he was trying to show that the structure of the world can be understood only through a radical epistemic dislocation.[2] The world was not as one thought it was but is not for that reason now fully lost. The kind of destruction of values that concerned Scheler implies, or maybe *indicts*, the very world in which that destruction proved to be possible. It is as if such a possibility had lain outside the thinkable until a certain historical time, but once it became thinkable, it was directly apprehended as a possibility of the world itself. Since the world was not understood to contain or imply such a possibility before (at least by some, or many), the world has proven to be different than it was. We can call it an altered world or a new world, but if we had a firm idea of the world in which certain events could not possibly happen, then it is surely now a different world than the one we thought we knew. This event introduces a possibility for many that is not like other such events and that could not be assimilated into an existing sense of the world. This possibility is not one that can be simply added to an existing idea of the world. Its addition changes the sense of the world; because it cannot be added as an attribute of an established world, it is upending and redefining, rife with the power to exhibit the world anew. This kind of "event"—to use Scheler's term—suddenly shows that the world had not been known before, even though it was there all along as a defining and framing horizon of experience. It may be useful to remember that for Husserl, in his *Nachlass*, and for Landgrebe, who early on sought to elucidate his doctrine, "to form an idea of the world requires, therefore, a systematic construction of the infinity of possible experiences."[3] So there is a question of whether any concept of the world can be definitively bounded, given an infinity of possibilities that cannot be fully conceptualized or imagined within a limit. Whatever limit is imposed by the notion of a horizon has to be rethought in terms of the infinity that, as it were, runs through and exceeds it.

WHY PHENOMENOLOGY? WHICH PHENOMENOLOGY?

The history of influence and appropriation in the field of phenomenology is complex. Both Merleau-Ponty and Sartre relied mainly on the French translations of Husserl, and they both borrowed from and contested his philosophical legacy. Sartre referred to the flesh briefly and in interesting ways, but most of his descriptions of the body tended to define it as an object among objects. Relying on a distinction between body and consciousness, he was subsequently called a Cartesian, and that was hardly a compliment, especially among those feminists who followed Simone de Beauvoir. For Beauvoir, the body is not an object but *a situation*. And when she introduces that notion in *The Second Sex*, it is not Sartre she cites but Merleau-Ponty.[4] Indeed, the problem of embodiment for feminist philosophy has given rise to an extensive scholarship in the relatively new field of critical phenomenology. Many scholars know the importance of the late Iris Marion Young's work.[5] She analyzes the habits and gestures of lived experience within a political frame, asking how "throwing like a girl" can be learned, how it becomes an obligatory lesson of gender, and how the hierarchical organization of gender is taken up and reproduced at the level of motility and gesture. Young's point, among others, is to foreground for feminist purposes the role of repeated and habitual actions in shaping bodies and worlds. For many other feminists of her generation (including myself), phenomenology opened a way to understand the structures of lived experience as they reflect upon and seek to transform structures of domination and discipline. The guiding aim of such scholarship is not to separate off a universal account of lived experience from particular social and historical structures but to show precisely how social structures are lived and, in the living, reproduced at the level of the body.

It is worth noting that Husserl and Merleau-Ponty played a formative role in the work of Sara Ahmed, Gayle Salamon, Lisa Guenther, and other feminist and critical phenomenologists. Even though Husserl thought that lived experience was structured in ways that were available to description, he was also aware of the sedimented character of lived experience that established its opacity as well as the changing historical frameworks within which life could be thought and lived which established its variability. Feminist phenomenologists, and now critical phenomenologists, have sought to derive from phenomenology a more precise way of understanding embodied life in its intersubjectivity which included the body's enmeshment with the powers of gender and racial formation, class, institutions, and even prisons, showing how power can be reproduced and contested in the tributaries of bodily movement, action, gesture, speech, suffering, passion, and resistance, to name but a few modalities of the body at issue.

Consider the description of critical phenomenology offered by one of the leading proponents of critical phenomenology, Lisa Guenther, who also works in the field of critical prison studies.[6] She writes, "By critical phenomenology I mean a method that is rooted in first-person accounts of experience but also critical of classical phenomenology's claim that the first-person singular is absolutely prior to intersubjectivity and to the complex textures of social life."[7] Thus, the transcendental subject that Scheler criticized received an even more powerful displacement here. Guenther provides a phenomenological analysis of prison strikes, especially the hunger strike, focusing on those who, in solitary confinement, rose up simultaneously in Palestine and California some years ago.[8] They could not gather, and their strike was not a work stoppage—they had no work. And yet they went on a hunger strike at the same time that a vast number lawyers and activists prepared the media strike, as it were. Although in absolute confinement, they made their demands known through a collaborative network, and they strengthened the mobilization against solitary confinement as cruel and unusual punishment. They also helped to vitalize an abolitionist movement led by women of color activists and scholars that indicts the entire prison system as institutional violence.[9]

Guenther demonstrates how phenomenology and politics are closely tied:

> One could approach the problem of mass incarceration as a dilemma to be solved through sentencing reform, legislative change, or even by releasing people from prison and eventually closing down prisons. But these ways of "solving" the dilemma of mass incarceration would not, in themselves, address the conditions of the problem's emergence, and they may actually exacerbate the problem by inscribing carceral logics more deeply, for example, by expanding non-custodial forms of surveillance and disciplinary control. In order to problematize mass incarceration, one must not only grasp how it is "wrong" and try to make it "right," one must trace the contingent, yet constitutive structures that normalize the conflation of accountability with punishment—and in order to do this, one must situate oneself in relation to networks of carceral power that promise security and prosperity to some, while exposing others to containment, control, and state violence.[10]

Here one can see how the phenomenological account of "naturalization"—how actions and gestures become normalized and taken for granted—is mobilized here. This analysis shows how imprisonment as accountability become taken for granted not only as a thought but as a practice. If we suspend our belief in that connection, if we denaturalize our understanding of prison—which is what the abolitionist imaginary requires— then we may see that this version of the world has been built or constituted through repeated acts that can be both analyzed and interrupted, and the processes formed by these iterable structures are brought to halt.

Here, again, queer theorist and critical phenomenologist Gayle Salamon, writing in "What's Critical About Critical Phenomenology?," puts it another way, showing how the visible world can hardly be taken for granted. For Salamon, the task of critical phenomenology is to open to the world or to reopen the world to a new consideration, and "that opening is revealed through the work of description."[11] Citing Foucault, she writes: "The role of philosophy is not to discover what is hidden, but to make visible precisely what is visible, that is to say, to make evident what is so close, so immediate, so intimately linked to us, that because of that we do not perceive it. Whereas the role of science is to reveal what we do not see, the role of philosophy is to let us see what we see."[12]

Although we might object to the ocular-centrism of that formulation, it foregrounds the importance of proximity that bears on all the senses. The problem of what has become established through time—through specific acts of constitution that "naturalize" the world, that is—make the current order of things appear timeless and necessary. One might consult also the enormously influential text by Sara Ahmed, *Queer Phenomenology: Orientations, Objects, Others* (2006), which uses the spatial orientations of phenomenology to think about queerness and sexual orientation more broadly—how we do, and do not, move through the world. That text takes as one of its points of departure Merleau-Ponty's views on embodiment and space in order to rethink, in Ahmed's own terms, what is meant by being oriented in space through and by relations to objects. Queer reading practices are thus derived from a critical reading of phenomenology itself. The critical phenomenology group—now represented by a journal, *Puncta*, and an impressive anthology, *Fifty Concepts for a Critical Phenomenology*[13]—describes itself as "foreground[ing] experiences of marginalization, oppression, and power in order to identify and transform common experiences of injustice that render 'the familiar' a site of oppression for many." Further, they invoke the metaphor of breath to describe their practice: they seek to "breathe new life into the phenomenological tradition and reveal its ethical, social and political promise." I suppose I have, unwittingly, joined them for the moment in this book as I wonder what use can be made of Merleau-Ponty's notion of "the intertwining" to understand our pandemic times.

BOUND UP WITH ONE ANOTHER

For Merleau-Ponty, human creatures, as bodily beings, are *in* the world at the same time that the world is *in us*, its objects encrusted onto us. The body does not appear as an object among objects. Although Husserl wrote about the structures of inter-subjectivity, Merleau-Ponty moved in another dimension, implying by his own descriptive language that philosophical understanding is better served by figures and appositions.[14] The intersubjective dimension of our lives, in his view, have to be understood as an "interlacing," an "overlapping," or perhaps through the rhetorical figure of *the chiasm*. The chiasm is that shared domain occupied by two distinct entities that, in every other respect, are quite clearly separate from each other. What the body is, then, is to some extent its relation to other bodies, and that relationality is to be thought as an ontological status that cannot be rightly understood through considering the body as substance; rather, relationality establishes and undoes the individual subject in the same stroke. This here is my hand that touches something or someone, but that touch is always of something that is either myself or another kind of being, which means that touching is "intentional" in the phenomenological sense: touching is always a touching *of* something. The object orientation of touch, even when it is oneself that is touched, defines touching and even retrospectively defines the phenomenological sense of the hand. This formulation indicates both the intentional and *worlded* character of touch. In other words, the tangible world is both its condition and its object, the basis for being a sensate being, what one senses, and a sense that exceeds any of its instances.

This last has some consequences for thinking ethics and perhaps compels a rethinking of reciprocity, which has been so important for theories of ethical obligation and social equality alike. If we extend Merleau-Ponty's understanding of our lives as implicated in one another's at the level of the body and the senses, then what I do, my very action, is mine, yes, but also always defined in relation to something that is not myself or, rather, myself as itself kind of alterity for the more active version of this "I." Within this framework, ethical conduct could not be described fully in the way that has been derived from Kant: I act according to a rule that everyone should adopt as the rule for their action, or I act in such a way that I can, without contradiction, will that others act the same way. In those hypothetical scenes, the other acts like me or should act like me if I am acting in the right way, and there is a parallelism between our actions, even an implicit form of reciprocity that assumes the duplication of action, yours and mine, in accord with the right rules or acts. Or I am oriented by the same rules as you are, and our common orientation toward that set of rules makes possible ethical conduct based on reciprocity. I act toward you as I would have you act toward me, which means that the same action is undertaken both personally and anonymously at the same time. Or the same kind of action is undertaken in accord with the same rule on both sides. The "I" and "you" proliferate in the course of such hypothetical variations, but what is the presumed relation between the "I" and the "you," these two sides of a bipolar relation, prior to being launched into the ethical scenario of deliberation? Can Kant give us direction here? And what if doing something to another is simultaneous with receiving the action of the other such that *doing* and *being done to* are not exactly distinct? If we say "touching you undoes me." then we are both reporting on an activity and an undergoing, and that undergoing is not a mere passivity but one bound up with an action whose origins are equivocal in an erotically important sense. As we elaborated in the prior chapters, the one who touches is also touched and also touches oneself, which means that there is an overlapping of my reflexive relation to myself and an intentional relation to another who also acts, even if not always in the same way or to the same degree. The two movements cross one another. And the site or time of their crossing is not only crucial for a phenomenology of erotic life but surely also part of what we might come to mean by a common world.

Remember that, in phenomenology, the term *intentional* does not mean deliberate or willful but the sense of being related to, oriented toward, an object as part of consciousness, attitude, or other modes of relationality. For Merleau-Ponty, then, we cannot subscribe to a methodological individualism and start with two distinct individuals, and neither can we easily subscribe to a strict distinction between activity and passivity. The reasons why have to do with how the body is implicated in the tangible and the tactile, the sensuous field, the visible, the aural in which other bodies are implicated as well. These fields are not exactly third terms or spheres that mediate among humans; they are the realms or fields implied by the senses. This and that tactile creature cross each other in that realm, and the realm is implied by their actions and is itself a kind of reciprocal crossing, a *chassé-croisé*. The relations are to be understood as chiasmic whenever we find each other touching the same surfaces and breathing proximate air; these domains of tactility or tangibility and respiration or breathability are both what we share and what we share differently, and also that which exceeds us and comprehends or embraces us at every instance of touch and breath. So although they are part of what is common between us, they are sites of division, vexation, and overlap than can be joyous or terrible. As such, the common is striated with both distinctness and overlap. A common world, as we know, does not mean that we share in it equally or that we are exposed to the same degree of toxicity or contagion. This is what Denise Ferreira da Silva refers to as "difference without separability."[15]

Merleau-Ponty sought to find a language that would challenge the epistemological exercise that presupposes the distance
between subject and object. He called intentionality an *embrace*
between the subject and world.[16] That was his way of redescrib-
ing the correlation between subjective structures of knowing
and the countervailing field of the knowable. Consciousness and
the world are suited for one another. Consciousness is equipped
with structures to know the world as it is, and the world gives
itself to consciousness to be known. This adequacy is part of a
medieval doctrine of intentionality and survives through the
phenomenological legacy.[17] I am not myself convinced by this,
but I appreciate the insistence on a harmonious embrace. It is a
lovely thought, but what if it turns out to be a chokehold that
deals pain rather than joy? What if consciousness and world are
singularly ill-suited for one another? Does it not depend on
which world, how its limits are established, and how its enduring "facts" are naturalized? Can we even distinguish the world
as such from this world, these worlds, striated with inequality,
ecological damage, and death-driven capitalism?

Merleau-Ponty's metaphors are pervasively erotic and harmonious. Even the "interlacing" does not seem like a bad deal. In
my view, Merleau-Ponty underestimates the rage that can
emerge from unstable forms of differentiation, although certainly he marked it in *Humanism and Terror*.[18] A psychoanalytic approach to differentiation would clearly imply a different
way of thinking about the boundaries of the body. Social theory can show how various ways of conceiving of the bounded
character of the body correlate with forms of individualism, but
psychoanalysis can give us a way of thinking about boundaries

as to some degree imaginary. The psychic fear of being without boundaries, fused with others, eradicated in one's distinctness has to be thought through in relation to the desire for boundaries, to shut down openings, to be fully defended or shielded. Freud's account of mass psychology is but one case in point, where social bonds are forged for destructive purposes.

The psychosocial dimensions of both individualism and fascism give us another way to think about "interlacing" and even the idealistic notion of the social bond as "an embrace." If we consider Merleau-Ponty's optimistic "embrace" as a way of thinking about the intentional relations to others and the world, it seems clear that it rules out or minimizes the possibility of violence, of erecting borders in the service of defense, both psychic and political. And yet the relation to dependency, and interdependency as well, is always haunted by irrecoverable impressions from infantile dependency, the long and failed struggle for complete differentiation from parental figures, the confusion about somatic boundaries that can just as easily lead to sexual violence or debilitating defensiveness. Although Merleau-Ponty was trained as a psychologist as well as a philosopher, there are moments in his text when a psychoanalytic rejoinder to his idealism seems necessary. Where is fantasy, loss, and the psychological disturbances that follow when the experience of the body as imago, or the bodily ego, contrasts with the lived experience at a distance. Frantz Fanon, who read Merleau-Ponty assiduously, knows this, bringing psychoanalysis to bear on his reading of phenomenological accounts of bodily life within racial imaginaries.[19]

■ ■ ■

Perhaps it is not possible to invoke the "we" as I have throughout this text, but it is meant as aspirational. An aspirational reading is one that seeks to breathe life into texts that have been read in fixed ways for too long, or that seeks to give new life through a text to a time that has been mired in anxiety and loss.[20] Or it is a way of hoping for "we" that does not yet exist. We are not fully distinct from each other (nor fully the same) for we are already implicated in each other's lives prior to any contract or consent. Further, we may rail against that fact and what it implies for the proximity, the interdependency, the inescapability of social relations themselves. Perhaps because we are interdependent when it comes to matters of survival and living on, or because we share a world of air and surface, breathing and touching, that we are commonly obligated to find a way to regulate matters such as air pollution, viral transmission, bodily contact, employment injury, sexual violation. Such regulations come at a cost that some are not willing to pay, those whose rights to destroy are bound up with their sense of personal freedom and the right to profit. These are all issues with which we have to deal because social and economic life is organized in specifically historical ways, and we have to struggle to exercise the power to further define those forms. At the same time, and presupposed by that very social organization, there are domains or zones or fields without which embodied life cannot be thought, including injurability, impressionability, passion, and susceptibility. Although we surely do object to the ways we are made *socially* vulnerable, that does not mean we can rule out bodily vulnerability. We can object to the kind of air we breathe and pass regulations—as we must—to keep it healthy for ourselves and for all life forms that depend on it, but no one can rule out the need for air to survive. Indeed, that requirement forms the basis of our claim, its first premise. Even if we say there are no primary needs that are not socially organized, that does not imply that those needs are the simple effects of social organization. This line of reasoning, I suggest, follows from a misunderstanding about the doctrine of social construction. When toxic environments enter into bodies, becoming part of their formation, their growth and biological organs such as bones and lungs are then affected; we are referring to the social construction of bodies and sometimes to the social construction of sex. This is not a fiction imposed upon a surface but a way in which the environment enters into our very bodies and determines our prospects for living.[21]

What we call primary requirements or needs are always socially organized but not, for that reason, socially generated in full. On the contrary, the need and requirement prompt social organization, and the two emerge together, but precisely because there are many ways to socially organize needs, we see the divergence between need and its social organization. Perhaps the word "need" is also unnecessary, and there is another way to designate primary requirements for life, conditions that must be met for the continuation or persistence of life, but the fact that we have to search for a word implies that something is there to be named. My wager is that Marx's *Economic and Philosophic Manuscripts of 1844* is one place to pursue this question.[22]

And yet Merleau-Ponty leads us away from a subject-centered account of basic needs. He does not ask what a single human subject requires but notes the requirement of sociality that emerges from embodied engagements with the world when the sensuous dimensions of the world take up the subject in the course of its formation. Hence, when we refer to touch, we are not only concerned with the subject capable of touch, the subject who consents to being touched, or the subject who seeks to find another through touch, although these are all crucial topics. Touch is in some ways subsumed under the tentacular in ways described by Bruno Latour, Isabelle Stengers, and Donna Haraway.[23] For Merleau-Ponty, the tangible takes us up in its grip: the visible is a field that orchestrates my seeing in relation to being seen. This unwieldy reversibility shows itself again when my reflexivity overlaps with a relation to others and to objects—and their relation to me. The field in which we act may at first appear as a third term that mediates between subject and other, but, in fact, it disarticulates the subject/object dichotomy as it traverses them both. Indeed, *the world* may well prove to be such a term as well, and all these fields to which I have referred may be ways in which the world exhibits its possibilities—in and through the senses and bodily experience now redefined as an inextricable implication in the sensuous dimensions of others, living creatures, objects, and the vexed and striated world in common.

If we are, as it were, mired in each other, or if our lives imply other lives that are equally dependent on domains of touch and breath, then when I pose the ethical question of how best to live under the pandemic, I have to reorient myself beyond both individualism and nationalism as well as white supremacy. Beginning with this scene of mutual implication, I then ask how to act and what to do in situations like the pandemic, I see that my doing is already bound up with yours, which means that my doing is not only mine, and although we are surely distinct, there is no easy escape from this relation of mutual implication. One reason for that interrelation is that we depend on and share the fields of the tangible, the visible, the breathable, and the edible and ingestible as well as the requirement for shelter and assistance of various kinds, including health care and life-enabling infrastructure. Of course, dependency can be miserable; it can take form as exploitation, imprisonment, and legal dispossession; it can be the scene of domination or unwanted self-loss. In those cases, reciprocity vanishes, as do ideals of equality. So the task is less a simple affirmation of interdependency than a collective effort to find or forge the best form of interdependency, the one that most clearly embodies the ideals of radical equality.

Is ethics to some extent a matter of acknowledging these bonds and partially shared dependencies on these conditions of life and living, ones that exist prior to any deliberate actions, that form the horizon within which such deliberations should take place? Even if the bonds are conceived as part of a social ontology, this does not mean they can be presumed as actualized. On the contrary, our task is to establish, as if the first time, a reciprocal relation that dissolves into neither self-interest nor communitarianism (the alibi for racism), nor national identity (the alibi for border violence and racism). The task would be to rethink ethical relationality as interlacing, or overlapping, or even as chiastic at the same time that we imagine equality in light of that background. The distinct "I" would retain its singularity but would no longer be the ground of such an ethic. No, that kind of ground is produced by a denial of interdependence and relationality and so must be upended.

I began this book by returning to Scheler briefly in order to pose the question *which value, or set of values, is destroyed in the world-formation called tragic?* I suppose that the pandemic led me to Scheler in part because it is the destruction of the equal value of lives as an ideal that seems to be happening, or is often at risk of happening, in these times. The destruction of value that takes place when lives are taken or destroyed, or left to die under conditions of preventable death, is the value of life, a value that only makes sense in light of the claim that *all* lives are equal or should be treated equally. That may seem paradoxical since the value of this or that life, as gleaned from memorials and memoirs, often relies on the singularity of that life and its value. For that reason, some fear that the assertion of equal value would threaten the singular value of this or that life, presuming that value is to be found in singularity. And yet when a number of people are killed by attacks, bombings, accidents, and illness, public mourning should follow and lost lives should be valued. The value lost is often considered as one that is shared or that somehow belongs to the people as a group. It is surprisingly difficult to talk about the value of life or lives in this way, since *value* as a term has been so thoroughly co-opted by market and financial *value*. Some of the obituaries of people lost in accidents, for instance, rely on forms of value generation that come from human capital, as when the depth and value of the loss is linked to a person's accomplishments and potential for generating future value or future generations, implicating predicting what the appreciation of their value as a person over time might have been.[24] We rarely see public obituaries extolling the person who lost their job or was unable for various reasons to do much of anything at all that could be affirmed by neoliberal metrics. If the person is a woman, she is quickly framed by the domestic sphere where her value consists in raising children or looking out for neighbors. Market and neoliberal values cannot communicate the value of lives lost since they are part of the machinery of loss itself, vectors for the death drive that prioritizes the value of markets at the expense of the lives that keep them open.

In chapter 1 I talk about the metric of value by which industries and universities proceed under pandemic conditions and the silent or vocalized calculations that are made about which deaths. How many deaths constitute a reasonable price to pay for the revitalization of markets? What are the values animated in such calculations, and what values are destroyed, leading to the exclamation *what kind of world is this?*, giving rise to the indictment of that world, the urgent call to animate or renew a different sense of world governed by another set of collective values?

The question of reasonable death rates is usually posed by those who do not consider themselves a possible factor in the equation. The one who calculates the acceptable level of death does not generally appear within the furnished statistics as a mortal creature who is potentially countable among the dead. The act of calculating seems to lift that human creature out of the sphere of finitude and produce a separate group of others whose lives and deaths can be calculated. Calculation seems to save the calculator from a calculable death—at least in the domain of fantasy. Indeed, does calculation of morbidity not always carry with it a dimension of fantasy? What we might call a post-sovereign or neo-sovereign form of calculation gives rise to a form of inequality that itself relies upon a metric of grievability—whose life, if lost, would count as a loss, enter into the registers of loss, even broach the status of an incalculable loss. And whose death can be quietly calculated without ever being named as such. In such instances, social inequality works together with necropolitical violence.

It would have laid out a clear path to resistance had the pandemic only etched firmly into public consciousness the contours of inequality within our institutions, households, and public spheres, exacerbating for many the lived sense of peril associated with the workplace, the home, and the street. And it would have marked out another path of political mobilization had the pandemic simply and clearly underscored the necessity of climate justice and rallied people across the globe to join in that impressive and urgent movement. But whatever politics we are building now must bring together those two issues to oppose both forms of destruction.[25] Further, the communities of care that have emerged during this pandemic have constituted new, life-giving social forms, expanding the notion of shelter beyond the household and the nation, and the same could be said about the public art now online that had us listening and watching in new ways. But the police violence against Black and brown people, women and men, trans people, the Indigenous and *travestis* in places like Brazil and the Andes, or on unceded land in the United States and Canada, coincides with the systematic forms of allowing death, promoted and accepted by market enthusiasts who operate under the guise of economic realism.

One proposal is to pursue a responsible capitalism in a pandemic that does not abandon vulnerable groups or that makes sure that such groups can sequester in ways that protect their immune systems. But this is not enough. I surely understand the effort to identify "vulnerable groups"—those who are especially likely to suffer the virus as a ravaging and life-threatening disease and to contrast them with those who are not at risk of losing their lives from the pathogen. The vulnerable include Black and brown communities deprived of adequate health care throughout their lifetimes and the history of this nation, the poor, the migrant, the incarcerated, the disabled, trans and queer people who struggle to achieve rights to health care, and all those with prior illnesses and enduring medical conditions. The pandemic exposes the heightened vulnerability to the illness of all those for whom health care is neither accessible nor affordable. The point, however, is not to sequester such groups but to create and sustain the conditions for their equal power and rights of belonging. To do this, market values can never be the guide. Those who exclaim with happiness during Omicron that "only 2,000 people every day are dying!" point to a number they are not only willing to accept but are utterly thrilled to champion.

Perhaps there are at least two provisional remarks about vulnerability that follow: it describes a shared condition of social life, of interdependency, exposure and porosity; it names the greater likelihood of dying for those who are marginalized, understood as the fatal consequence of a pervasive social inequality. Yes, many who have died under Omicron are unvaccinated, but antivax sentiment is only partially responsible for those deaths. There are good reasons why many would distrust the missives that come from necropolitical governments, and some have little access to vaccine education or to vaccines, and for some vaccines cannot work, given their immunological compromise. Triumphant utilitarianism is just another way of saying "let them die."

Chapter 4

GRIEVABILITY FOR THE LIVING

IN MY book *The Force of Nonviolence* (2020), I argue that the distinction between the grievable and the ungrievable is part of the very operation and meaning of social and economic inequality but also the effect, if not the expression, of violence.[1] What does it mean to be grievable? We may think that someone or something lost is grievable or ungrievable by which we mean that it is either publicly marked and acknowledged or it passes without a trace, with no, or little, acknowledgment. Of course, a smaller group may grieve a loss with intensity and duration, but the loss and the mourning do not show up on the dominant radars tracking human value. Arguments such as mine depend on a conception of "acknowledgment" that may seem ambiguous. I draw on Freud's argument in "Mourning and Melancholia" that mourning consists of acknowledgment of loss, of registering the reality of loss and undoing the ramparts of defense against knowing the event of loss itself. Acknowledgment of this kind is a struggle that takes time, a syncopated effort to touch upon a loss repeatedly that may be difficult to fathom or accept. Freud claims that it usually happens bit by bit as different moments of reality confirm that someone or something is irreversibly gone. Only in time do we come to see or feel that someone is really gone; in Freud's language, the "verdict of reality" is delivered over time as the not-thereness of the person is marked in different situations.² In phenomenological language, one might say that a person is now present only in the mode of being irreversibly gone. Melancholia, for Freud, is often described as the failure to acknowledge that a loss has happened, usually a form of denial unconsciously and fiercely held that takes outward form as complaint, despondency, or self-vilification.

The difference, then, between mourning and melancholy seems to turn on the question of acknowledgment. Since *Gender Trouble*, I have sought to extend the analysis of melancholia beyond the individual psyche to understand as a broader cultural form that takes hold when certain kinds of losses cannot be marked or valued. Under conditions where one's love or attachment cannot be acknowledged and one loses that love, one can acknowledge neither the love nor the loss. And that leaves a person in a melancholic condition, one that includes elements of both depression and mania or is characterized precisely by the oscillation between the two.³ When considering melancholia, it matters *what* one loses; it can be a person or the love of that person, but Freud is clear that it can be an ideal, a fantasy of who that person should have been, or indeed an ideal of a nation. The loss of white demographic advantage in various U.S. states implies that white supremacists have to lose their fantasy of supremacy, an ideal that was never possible and should have never been entertained. As they rail against equality, they refuse a loss that they are now compelled to mourn. Let us hope they finish that process soon.

Earlier in my career I suggested that gender itself may be partially constructed through melancholia to the extent that some versions of cis-masculinity depend upon the denial of any love for other men. For some, to be a man means precisely never having loved another man and never having lost a man.[4] This "never having" loved and lost is a denial that gets built into the gender at issue, a melancholic formation that forms an unconscious bond among those who dwell in that version of masculinity. Similarly, the claim that one would never be gay and never have been gay is a kind of protest suggesting that another voice coming from elsewhere is promoting a countervailing view. The protest deflects the acknowledgment of a loss, but it may also be read as a disfigured form of acknowledgment. What if feelings of gay desire were regarded as relatively common, "endemic" to the social fabric? One question I asked decades ago was whether gender melancholia of this sort has a certain cultural generality, and whether we might speak of a cultural melancholia, one that is commonly found among straight men whose masculinity depends more or less on a steadfast denial of the mere thought of their possibly gay desires. Of course, we know that a wide range of masculinities exist in cis-, queer, and trans life that do not correlate with this kind of denial, but perhaps there is one normative sort that still fits the profile. At the time, I was in part guided by the study authored by Alexander Mitscherlich and Margarete Mitscherlich, *The Inability to*

Mourn, which documents a pervasive melancholia in German culture during the postwar years.[5] It appears that they could not acknowledge or mourn their own losses or, indeed, their own destructiveness, and yet they were haunted by experiences of destruction and loss that they could not quite name. The rush to move beyond the Nazi years into the economic boom of the 1950s brought with it a mania for the market and its specific sense of futurity, along with a pervasive sense of depression, what Freud—following early modern precedents—had called melancholia, now emerging as a cultural condition.

In recent years, I've tried to think about wars and public attacks on human life and asked the question *whose life is a candidate for public mourning, and whose is not?*[6] It struck me as significant then that the United States never mourns those they kill but only its own citizens, and mainly those who are white and propertied and married more easily than those who are poor, queer, Black or brown, or without papers. Living humans bear a sense of whether they belong to the grievable classes, as it were. To say of a living person that they are grievable is to say that they would be grieved were they to be lost. It is also to say that the world is, or should be, organized to sustain that life, to support the open-ended future of that life. And those who live with the sense that there is no certainty about food or shelter or health care also live with a sense of their dispensability. Living with a somatic sense of dispensability is the feeling that one could die and pass from the earth leaving no mark and without acknowledgment. It is a lived conviction that one's own life does not matter to others or, rather, that the world is organized—the economy is organized—so that the lives of some will be safeguarded and the lives of others will not. When the economy starts up following a pandemic surge, knowing full well that some people will die, a class of dispensable people is being identified and created. This is a fascist moment that emerges amid a market calculation, and we are living in a time when this form of calculation threatens to become the norm. It is, in fact, a rationality and a power that we must fight at quotidian and global levels.

Thus, to live as someone with a sense of being ungrievable is to understand that one belongs to that class of the dispensable and to feel abandonment as basic institutions of care either pass one by, once again, or are withdrawn. One is oneself the loss that cannot be mourned. This kind of melancholia belongs to the sense of foreclosed futurity that goes along with having perpetually fallen through a safety network, perhaps burdened with unpayable debt, in pursuit of elusive health care, or subject to sporadic housing and uncertain income. If this life is not regarded as worthy of safeguarding, then is this a life without value? Or has "value" itself been hijacked by a metric whose value we must radically question? And what sense of value is, and should be, accorded to lives, and to what metric does it belong?

I have argued that it is not possible to understand social inequality without understanding how grievability is unequally distributed. That unequal distribution is a key component of social inequality, one that generally has not been taken into account by social theorists. It follows that the designation, whether explicit or implicit, of a group or population as ungrievable means that they can be targeted for violence or left to die without consequence. Such a targeting can be implied by a set of policies and theories and does not have to be discovered as the deliberate wish of any social actor. Hence, the kind of social inequality established by differential grievability qualifies as a form of institutional violence. In my view, the struggle for a nonviolent politics is at once a struggle for the equal value of lives and against the lethal logics, the necro-political metrics, that continue to mark (or leave unmarked) populations as dispensable, lives as not worth safeguarding, lives as not worth mourning. To recapitulate the two parts of my argument: (1) The struggle against social inequality has to be a struggle against differential grievability; and (2) This struggle is also part of a nonviolent politics. For nonviolence is not only opposing this or that act of violence, but violent institutions and policies and states that adopt as their policy the targeting of populations for death or policies for letting people die in conditions of duress. We can think here, surely, about the European Union's cruel policy toward migrants and its hideous criminalization of humanitarian actors who seek to preserve the lives of those seeking to cross the Mediterranean when nation-states refuse.

Under conditions of pandemic, it may be that we are all suffering from some version of melancholia. How does it become possible to mourn so many people? Do any of us know how to name what we have lost? What kind of public mark or monument would begin to address this need to mourn? Everywhere we sense the absence of the mark, the gap within the sensible world. Where gatherings are themselves highly restricted and are anxious or intermittent and designed as a way to mourn, what ways are left to connect? Many have now attended the Zoom memorials and know the difficulty of this practice. The inability to see someone close in a hospital before they die, the inability to gather with those who knew that person, these make for truncated experiences of loss where acknowledgment cannot happen openly and communally with ease. Many people who have suffered loss have been returned to the household as the exclusive site for mourning, deprived of more public gatherings in which such losses are marked and commonly registered. The internet has more fully claimed its place as the new public sphere, but it can never fully substitute for those gatherings, both private and public, that allow losses to be fathomed and lived through with one another. And if we do gather, we keep our distance, strain to hug in awkward ways, kiss with a generalized sense of anxiety. And in the spring of 2022, memorial gatherings became another place where people contracted the virus. A purely private form of mourning is possible, but can it release or assuage the open cry, the stories, the songs that petition the world to bear witness to this loss in its singularity within a social fabric of interwoven lives? As is the case with public losses of such magnitude and quick succession, there are always political questions that are linked with the demand for public mourning. Earlier in the pandemic, the images of bodies piled high in Ecuador or stacked in closets in New Jersey or Northern Italy let us know in graphic terms how overwhelmed and underfunded the infrastructure of hospitals have been, deprived of the power to care for those in distress. Too often the images of the dead and dying flit by as sensational clips. Sequestering enforces both a sense of ambient death and a shared practice of deflection: "let's not focus on the negative!" The task, though, is to convert that ambient sense of loss into mourning and demand. Learning to mourn mass death means marking the loss of someone whose name you do not know, whose language you may not speak, who lives at an unbridgeable distance from where you live, insisting on a global frame for our disorientation. One does not have to know the person lost to affirm that *this was a life*. One does not have to have all the details about a life to know that it existed. The right to belong to the world is anonymous but no less obligatory for that reason. In public discourse, it is the life cut short, the life that should have had a chance to live more, that captures our attention. The elderly are on their way to death (and the rest of us are not?). Whatever the age, the value of that person is now carried in the lives of others, a form of acknowledgment that becomes an incorporation, a living echo, an animated wound or trace that transforms those who live on. Just because someone else suffers in a way that I have not suffered does not mean that the other's suffering is unthinkable to me. Our bonds are forged from echoes, translation, and resonances, rhythms, and repetitions, as if the musicality of mourning makes its way past borders by virtue of its acoustic powers. The loss that the stranger endures echoes with the personal loss one feels, even as it is not the same. Because it is not the same, it echoes. An interval becomes a link. Strangers in grief nevertheless have formed a kind of collectivity.

The modes of market calculation and speculation that have accepted death for many as the price to pay for supporting the "health" of the market are accepting the sacrifice of some lives as a reasonable price, a reasonable norm. And, yes, such a consequence has come to qualify as "reasonable" within that particular rationality. Because market rationality does not exhaust rationality, because the calculating rationality founders on its own limit, we can—even without a firm or single definition of life—assert the incalculable value of lives. The quandary is to construe a notion of social equality that incorporates rather than negates that incalculable value.

It was, in fact, in Jacques Derrida's reading of Husserl's *Crisis of the European Sciences* that he derives the incalculable value of life through recourse to Kant. In seeking to understand "the possibility of an incalculable that is neither irrational nor dubitable," Derrida suggests

> that a rational and rigorous incalculability presented itself *as such* in the greatest tradition of rationalist idealism. The rationality of the rational has never been limited, as some have tried to make us believe, to calculability, to reason as calculation, as *ratio*, as account, an account to be settled or an account to be given. . . . The role that "dignity" (*Würde*), for example, plays in the *Groundwork of the Metaphysics of Morals* belongs to the order of the incalculable. In the kingdom of ends, it is opposed to what has a price on the market (*Marktpreis*) and so can give rise to calculable equivalences. The dignity of a reasonable being (the human person, for example, and this is, for Kant, the only example) is incalculable as an end in itself.[7]

Although I wish that Kant had invoked this argument to challenge his support for the death penalty (where he argued that our lives belong to the state and so can be justifiably taken away by the state[8]), we can turn his view in a more Arendtian direction. Remember that Hannah Arendt told us that Adolf Eichmann had no right to decide with whom he would cohabit the earth.[9] He could not say that he wanted to live in a world without Jews or any other group of living humans since that choice is not given to humans. Humans, according to Arendt, lack any such right, and when they seek to obliterate a group of people from the earth, they are exercising a genocidal prerogative for which there is no justification. For Arendt, human creatures are born into a condition of common cohabitation, marked by a persistent heterogeneity or plurality, and this given plurality is the horizon within which we choose and act. But if we act against this given plurality, we commit a crime against the very condition of human life, understood as a social and political life. Of course, we may not love or savor the connections into which we are born—very few of us actually get to choose our families, for example. But the obligations of cohabitation are not always born from love or even choice; the relations between us, this sociality goes beyond kinship, community, nation, and territory. It takes us, rather, in the direction of the world. Of course, Arendt's well-known love of the world may well name this disposition to secure the conditions of cohabitation, but even then, what do we make of the enormous potential we carry to destroy that upon which we depend for life itself? What kind of creatures are we, or what kind of creatures have we become, who can so easily destroy the conditions of our own living?

I have suggested that interdependency describes a condition of life awkwardly and necessarily shared—the perils and passions of bodily exposure, of porosity, taking or letting something in, letting something out, existing, as it were, in that threshold and through such passages. When social inequality implies a greater likelihood of dying, then the portal to the future is opened by more radical and substantive social equality, a more mindful form of collective freedom, and a mass mobilization against violence in its explicit and fugitive forms. If we seek to repair the world or, indeed, the planet, then the world must be unshackled from the market economy that traffics and profits from its distribution of life and death. A politics of life would not be the reactionary one, nor would it reduce to a simple vitalism. Rather, it would be a critical reflection on the shared conditions of life for the purposes of realizing a more radical equality and honoring a nonviolent mandate of a global character. Perhaps this is a way to begin the world again, even as that world is already under way, to repair forward, as it were, as a new imaginary emerges from the hauntings of the present, the liminal horizon of this world.

POSTSCRIPT

TRANSFORMATIONS

I HAVE noted that one might expect that a consideration of grievability pertains only to those who are dead, but my contention is that grievability already operates in life as a characteristic attributed to living creatures, those who walk around knowing that their lives, or those they love, may well vanish at any moment, and without a proper mark or protest. Some know already that they will be, or may be, subject to early and violent death, and the day goes on in the shadow of that conviction. Consider the sudden or gradual collapse of the world that necessitates flight, trusting the horrible stranger to move one's family across the Mediterranean, a guy with a profit motive and a poorly crafted vessel, only to be pushed back by Maltese authorities, or to capsize without hope of rescue, or to be discovered by the Italian or Greek coast guard and to enter into an indefinite time of detention, or to face the impossibility of transit, brutally closed borders, unsanitary conditions, denial of national and international rights, and repeated questions of how to survive, to move, and to arrive, and how to do all this with others who are caught in the same situation.

I have suggested that grievability is a necessary condition for equality. It has to do with counting as a life, or, we may say, it has to do with being a body that matters. Thus, the assertion of grievability is one of the central claims of the Movement for Black Lives, one of the most powerful social movements of recent times, whose name is also a slogan. The slogan should not be underestimated as a political tool. We see this as well with ¡Ni Una Menos! (Not One Less!), a chant that became the name of a movement. An action that becomes the name designating a group that has gathered around an affectively invested signifier. And in both of these cases, the movements have traveled across borders even when so many people cannot pass.

My point here is twofold: the first is that the Movement for Black Lives is at once a form of public mourning, a form of gathering and nongathering, embodied and virtual, that crosses borders and is not itself subject to any lockdown. We might call the movement a counter-contagion. In recent months, every time police kill an unarmed Black person, a person who is in resting in her bed at home (Breonna Taylor), or running in the opposition direction (Walter Scott), or when white individuals kill a Black person taking a jog in the street (Ahmaud Arbery), tens of thousands of people take to the street to object to this murder. The name of one group, Black Lives Matter, communicates that Black lives cannot be extinguished so easily and arbitrarily; that the white supremacist devaluation of Black lives will be opposed every time it takes action; that in marking and mourning these lives, even if we did not know them, we are insisting that they should have lived more and longer; that these deaths were criminal acts; and that the police or other perpetrators should be held accountable or, indeed, that the police force itself should be dissolved.

A concrete set of political proposals emerges from the assertion of grievability. The politics of grievability, however, does not conclude with that assertion. Marking the loss is harder to do in the case of all those who are "left to die," abandoned to the virus without proper shelter or health care. Letting to die is also the tacit policy of market rationality that accepts a certain number of deaths as necessary to keep the economy going. The now vanished former president of the United States embraced herd immunity during his time in power, revivifying the spirit of eugenics and accepting that the strong and rich will survive and that those who are poor and apparently "weak," in his mind, will die. "Let [the virus] rip!" was one of his slogans, translating into "let everyone die who is going to die from this illness so that the economy stays healthy since the health of the economy is more important than the health of those most vulnerable"—a treacherous form of Malthusianism but also an exhilarated expression of a death drive that could have taken his own life, and almost did.

Like Black Lives Matter, Ni Una Menos has taken to the streets to oppose violence against women including domestic battery and rape, but its agenda is complex and introduces a new vision of the political: it opposes dictatorship, contemporary forms of revisionism, wage inequalities for women, femicide and rape, capitalist exploitation, and extractivism, and it also promotes radical democracy in the form of open parliaments and assemblies that decide on common actions, recalling the spontaneous parliaments that emerged on the streets of Argentina after the last dictator fell. It survives the pandemic lockdown by extending its solidarities cross-regionally and online as well as through new publications and new forms of gathering online. Of course, Ni Una Menos not only took *to* the streets but took *over* the streets, making it impossible for police to be on the streets in Argentina. Similar gatherings flooded the streets of Ecuador, Chile, Colombia, Puerto Rico, and Mexico, and the movement, including its proposal of a feminist strike, moved to Italy and Turkey. Those large gatherings (sometimes as many as three million gathered in the streets in Latin America) required large and close gatherings that cannot happen now, but what continues to happen is (a) reflection on the movement, its past, and its future, and (b) the publication of books, including the English publication of Verónica Gago's *The Feminist International*, which lays out the terms of the feminist strike both as an event and an ongoing collective process.[1] A political movement is never just the event of its gathering. We see this as networks are formed, and reading and writing become themselves part of a feminist revolutionary project. In pandemic times, it is especially important to remember Gago's view, which reanimates the political thought of Rosa Luxemburg, that the strike always exceeds the act or the event, marking a vector of temporalities from which a new temporal horizon emerges or can emerge. The slogans and the gatherings start to articulate this new sociality, and for Gago, the "gestures of revulsion" are key to both uprising and strike.[2] Women leave their homes for the street, and even though many women have been forced back into domestic enclosures, there are still ways of forging links and continuing to build social connections that foreshadow or prefigure future forms. For Gago, the feminist strike is linked with the general assembly, the *assemblea*, which is the understood as "a situated apparatus of collective intelligence," which means both a site and practice for thinking together about common problems but also about the common world to be built.[3] Revising the legacy of Rosa Luxemburg for our times, Gago links the praxis of revolution to the critique of finance under neoliberalism, colonial dispossession, and patriarchal forms of state terrorism directed against women, trans, *travestis*, precarious workers, and the Indigenous. A wide number of theories and practices come to bear upon this intellectual work but also a set of transregional collaborations that do not rely on gathering or assembly at every turn. Indeed, for an analysis to be transregional and transversal, it cannot in principle require the physical gathering.

What is most important in these days are actions that keep the relationship between affect and action alive, that turn revulsion and outrage into the collective potential and revolutionary promise. It is only through the cumulative power of small acts of labor that revolutionary potential is kept alive. Equally important is the demand to keep life alive—that is, to demand the conditions for living, which includes the end to the murdering of women, Black and brown people, trans and queer people, and all those who are punished or disappeared because of their political affiliations. The opposition to sexual violence is thus linked with the violence perpetrated by the state under both dictatorship and neoliberal financial regimes.

No grand demonstration ever worked without working behind the scenes. As Alicia Garza makes clear about Black Lives Matter (and she coined that term), the work of politics consists of painstaking and committed forms of making alliances so that when the event comes, the gathering will be immediate and focused. Every gathering is conditioned and exceeded by its network of alliance, and the entirety of a network never appears at once.

And alliance is part of what we saw emerging in 2020 and 2021 with mutual aid societies, nonnuclear pods, and expanding networks of care.[4] *The Care Manifesto*, written collaboratively by feminist activists and authors in London, asks us to consider care not as a private and sequestered activity but as a form of power with the potential to change global practices and institutions and to transform the world. Setting aside speculation about the essential feminine, the call to "care" resonates with Gago's revolutionary feminism by launching a bracing critique of neoliberal profit-making. *The Care Manifesto* links the transformation of kinship with the gendered division of labor and ecological activism, and does this through recourse to the feminist ideal of interdependence that moves beyond the dyadic model to a cross-weaving of intersubjectivity itself.[5] Authors Catherine Rottenberg and Lynne Segal insist that the capacity for reflection amid urgent times is a political necessity.[6] They also bring forward some of the psychoanalytic complexities of care and care work by reminding us that, etymologically, care comes from *caru*, a term that includes concern, anxiety, sorrow, grief, *and trouble*.[7]

Although Merleau-Ponty does not, I think, make a showing, the argument is clear that care implicates us in each other's lives, mapping and animating a politics of promise for our times. It is exemplified in the care networks that operate outside of government offices and structures that offer transportation, food delivery, and shelter to those in need, and that widen circles of support through online networks that produce material effects, constituting new social infrastructures in the face of failing or absent ones. The normative principles for this movement include, as I said, interdependency, social solidarity, and revolutionary critique. They are seeking to provide the conditions for life, for living on, for living together. The care solidarities are opposed to brutal murder and to letting people die. And in the case of both Black Lives Matter and Ni Una Menos, the opposition to killing as a moral obligation only takes substantial form once it is linked with a broader critique of, and opposition to, institutional inequality and exploitation.[8]

I would simply add that once we recognize the unequal distribution of the grievability of lives, our debates about equality and violence will be transformed, and the link between the two domains, more firmly understood. For equality and livability to become pervasive features of our world, they must be asserted and claimed by precisely those bodies who endeavor still to live, to secure the conditions of living, whose living endeavor becomes the very substance of thought—and of transformative protest.

In the North American winter of 2022, as the Delta variant subsided and Omicron spiked (before Deltacron emerged), it was clear that the celebrations that proclaimed the pandemic to be over were more hopeful than realistic. Given that many countries and regions have seen very few vaccines, it is more important than ever to understand how global inequalities, mired in racism, establish the positions from which the history of the pandemic can be narrated. In the United States and the United Kingdom, the media reports increasing levels of anger among the population who consider it to be their "right" to be done with the pandemic and to return to lives pursued in accord with their personal liberty. The manic glee that followed from the eradication of all precautions in the United Kingdom seemed to be a celebration of the personal liberty to move freely in crowds at the expense of those who remain unprotected, and without concern for the long-term consequences that can follow contracting Covid-19. This form of liberty is expressed as righteous entitlement, the right to throw off the state and its health mandates, the right to get sick and to make others sick, the right to spread death if that is one's wish, if spreading death is the expression of personal liberty.

Vladimir Putin would surely agree that destruction is the ultimate sign of personal power, if not liberty. The rage is the voice of personal liberty as it abandons a common or shared life, the ideals of collective freedom, and the care for the earth and for living creatures, including human ones. The rage may be the last gasps of a version of personal liberty that understood personhood to be bound by the skin—discrete and separate—a fantasy of closing all the apertures except for the purposes of furthering consumption and pleasure for the individual, a fantasy that what lets the world in is one's choice and what we put into the world can be regulated and determined by oneself alone. Such "individuals" imagine themselves separate from toxic air and soil, from microbes and bacteria. As porous, the body is neither pure boundary nor pure opening but a complex negotiation among the two, situated in a mode of living where breath, food, digestion, and well-being—for sexuality, intimacy, and the taking in of each other's bodies—are all requirements (for oneself, of and by the world). We cannot really live without each other, without finding ourselves inside another's pores, or without letting another in. For that is where we live, outside of the bounded self and its conceits, as an opening toward the world. We live, that is, in relation to a world that sustains us, an earth and its habitats, including human ones, that depend on a politics that is committed to a world in which we can all breathe without fear of contagion, fear of pollution, or fear of the police chokehold, where our breath is intermingled with the world's breath, where that exchange of breath, syncopated and free, becomes what is shared—our commons, as it were.

NOTES

INTRODUCTION

1. Stefano Harney and Fred Moten, *The Undercommons: Fugitive Planning and Black Study* (New York: Minor Compositions, 2013), https://www .minorcompositions.info/wp-content/uploads/2013/04/undercommons -web.pdf.
2. Harney and Moten, *Undercommons*.
3. Jacques Rancière, *Dissensus: On Politics and Aesthetics*, trans. Steven Corcoran (London: Continuum, 2010), 33.
4. "Hospitalization and Death by Race/Ethnicity," COVID-19, Centers for Disease Control and Prevention, last modified June 17, 2021, https://www .cdc.gov/coronavirus/2019-ncov/covid-data/investigations-discovery /hospitalization-death-by-race-ethnicity.html.
5. "Vaccine Nationalism & The Political Economy of the COVID-19 Vaccines," The Moldova Foundation, published March 9, 2021, https://www .moldova.org/en/vaccine-nationalism-the-political-economy-of-covid -19/.
6. Hans-Georg Gadamer's theorization of "horizons" of understanding can be found in *Truth and Method*, trans. Joel Weinsheimer and Donald G. Marshall (New York: Bloomsbury, 2013).

7. Sindre Bangstad and Tobjørn Tumyr Nilsen, "Thoughts on the Planetary: An Interview with Achille Mbembe," *New Frame*, September 5, 2019, https://www.newframe.com/thoughts-on-the-planetary-an-interview -with-achille-mbembe/.

8. Bangstad and Nilsen, "Thoughts on the Planetary" (my emphasis).

9. Christopher Prendergast, ed. *Debating World Literature* (London: Verso, 2004); and Emily Apter, *Against World Literature: On the Politics of Untranslatability* (London: Verso, 2013). See also Deborah Dankowski and Eduardo Viveiros de Castro, *The Ends of the World*, trans. Rodrigo Nunes (Cambridge, Mass.: Polity Press, 2017).

10. María Lugones, "Playfulness, 'World'-Travelling, and Loving Perception," *Hypatia* 2, no. 2 (1987): 3–19.

11. See, for instance, the website "Parasites Without Borders" for a light but serious effort to provide scientific education for those who have the power to alleviate suffering wherever it occurs: https://parasiteswithoutborders .com/daily-covid-19-updates/.

12. See Thomas Pradeu, *The Limits of the Self: Immunology and Biological Identity*, trans. Elizabeth Vitanza (Oxford: Oxford University Press, 2012). Pradeu argues against the immunological framework that accepts a self/ non-self dichotomy in favor of a continuity thesis that emphasizes reactive patterns and memories in the organism's immune system, as it were. Thus, the impress and intrusion of the external world helps to structure the organism and its responsiveness. Pradeu underscores that immunological challenges to that system can be endogenous or exogenous and that what constitutes a challenge is a rupture in the established patterns of interaction. Thus, the problem is not the acceptance or rejection of what is foreign but the creation of new patterns of interactivity in the wake of unprecedented challenges to that system. Therefore, the virus of Covid-19 is not a problem of foreign-ness, as those who call it "the China virus" imply, but of the unprecedented. As something new, it demands that our systems become new as well. See also Thomas Pradeu, *The Philosophy of Immunology* (Cambridge: Cambridge University Press, 2020), https:// www.cambridge.org/core/elements/philosophy-of-immunology/06FoC3 41035299674EECF0406E5D8E31, where he reminds us that bacteria from the external world is part of digestion, functioning, and tissue repair. He further remarks that "defense" cannot be the defining or exclusive feature of immune systems since the functioning of the immune system not only depends upon "heterogeneous constituents" but requires them for the

integration of the self. Thus, integration only makes sense as a concept if heterogeneity is part of its very definition.

13. See, for instance, Anne Fausto-Sterling, *Sex/Gender: Biology in a Social World* (New York: Routledge, 2012).

14. According to Pradeu, "immunity has been understood historically as an organism's capacity to defend itself against pathogens, and that defensive immune mechanisms have been identified in all species . . . the immune system cannot be reduced to its defense activity and promote on this basis an extended view of immunity." He further argues that "the complexities of accounting for the evolution of immunological processes and attributing a single function to the immune system" suggest that defense is but only one factor in a complex and process characterized by discontinuity among its functions (*The Philosophy of Immunology*).

15. Ludwig Wittgenstein, *Tractatus Logico-Philosophicus*, trans. C. K. Ogden (Mineola, N.Y.: Dover, 1999), 6.43.

16. Wittgenstein, *Tractatus Logico-Philosophicus*.

17. Wittgenstein, *Tractatus Logico-Philosophicus*.

18. Martin Heidegger, "The Age of the World-Picture," in *The Question Concerning Technology and Other Essays*, trans. William Lovitt (New York: Harper & Row, 1977), 129.

19. Heidegger, "The Age of the World-Picture," 132–134.

1. SENSES OF THE WORLD

1. Sigmund Freud, *Reflections on War and Death*, trans. A. A. Brill and Alfred B. Kuttner (New York: Moffat Yard, 1918). The most accessible English version of this essay is "On the Tragic," in *The Questions of Tragedy*, ed. Arthur B. Coffin (San Francisco: Edwin Mellen Press, 1991), 105–126. However, citations in this article are from the same essay, published as Max Scheler, "On the Tragic," trans. Bernard Stambler, *Cross Currents* 4, no. 2 (Winter 1954): 178–191. My own translations from the German are marked as such and are taken from "Bemerkungen zum Phänomen des Tragischen," in Max Scheler, *Gesammelte Werke*, Band 3 (Franke Verlag, 2007), 277–302.

2. Ludwig Landgrebe, "The World as a Phenomenological Problem," *Philosophy and Phenomenological Research* 1, no. 1 (September 1940): 38–58.

3. Jean-Paul Sartre, *The Transcendence of the Ego: A Sketch for a Phenomenological Description*, trans. Andrew Brown (Milton Park, Abingdon, Oxon: Routledge, 2004); and Aron Gurwitsch, *Studies in Phenomenology and Psychology* (Evanston, Ill.: Northwestern University Press, 1966).

4. Edmund Husserl, *The Phenomenology of Internal Time Consciousness* (Bloomington: Indiana University Press, 1964), 98–128.

5. Scheler, "On the Tragic," 178 (my emphasis).

6. Scheler, "On the Tragic," 180.

7. Scheler, "On the Tragic," 182.

8. Scheler, "On the Tragic," 182.

9. Scheler, "On the Tragic," 182.

10. Scheler, "On the Tragic," 182; in German, 278.

11. Scheler, "On the Tragic," 182.

12. Scheler, "On the Tragic," 182.

13. Scheler, "On the Tragic," 187.

14. See https://blacklivesmatter.com/; and Barbara Ransby, *Making All Black Lives Matter: Reimagining Freedom in the Twenty-First Century* (Oakland: University of California Press, 2018); and Alicia Garza, *The Purpose of Power: How We Come Together When We Fall Apart* (New York: Penguin Random House, 2021).

15. Maurice Merleau-Ponty, "Eye and Mind," in *The Primacy of Perception and Other Essays on Phenomenological Psychology, the Philosophy of Art, History and Politics*, ed. James M. Edie, trans. Carleton Dallery (Evanston, Ill.: Northwestern University Press, 1964), 162–163.

16. Maurice Merleau-Ponty, "The Intertwining—The Chiasm," in *The Visible and the Invisible*, ed. Claude Lefort, trans. Alphonso Lingis (Evanston, Ill.: Northwestern University Press, 1968), 147, 148.

2. POWERS IN THE PANDEMIC

1. On climate change making pandemics more possible, see Damian Carrington, "World Leaders 'Ignoring' Role of Destruction of Nature in Causing Pandemics," *Guardian*, June 4, 2021, https://www.theguardian.com/world/2021/jun/04/end-destruction-of-nature-to-stop-future-pandemics-say-scientists; and Rasha Aridi, "To Prevent Future Pandemics, Protect Nature," *Smithsonian Magazine*, October 30, 2020, https://www.smithsonianmag.com/smart-news/protecting-nature-will-protect

-us-how-prevent-next-pandemic-180976177/. On lessons from the pandemic for opposing climate destruction, see David Klenert, Franziska Funke, Linus Mattauch, and Brian O'Callaghan, "Five Lessons from COVID-19 for Advancing Climate Change Mitigation," *Environmental and Resource Economics* 76 (2020): 751–778, https://doi.org/10.1007/s10640 -020-00453-w; and Krystal M. Perkins, Nora Munguia, Michael Ellenbecker, Rafael Moure-Eraso, and Luis Velasquez, "COVID-19 Pandemic Lessons to Facilitate Future Engagement in the Global Climate Crisis, *Journal of Cleaner Production* 290 (2021): 125178, https://doi.org/10.1016/j .jclepro.2020.125178.

2. An early and pointed articulation of the relationship between wage labor and the worker's immiseration under capitalism can be found in Marx's "Economic and Philosophic Manuscripts of 1844," in *Karl Marx / Frederick Engels Collected Works*, vol. 3, trans. Martin Milligan and Dirk Struik, 229–376 (New York: International Publishers, 1975).

3. Maurice Merleau-Ponty, "The Intertwining—The Chiasm," in *The Visible and the Invisible*, ed. Claude Lefort, trans. Alphonso Lingis, 130–155 (Evanston, Ill.: Northwestern University Press, 1968).

4. This point, resonant with Merleau-Ponty's explorations, is made persuasively by Gilles Deleuze in "What Can a Body Do?" in *Expressionism in Philosophy: Spinoza*, trans. Martin Joughin, 217–234 (New York: Zone, 1992).

5. See María Lugones, "Playfulness, 'World'-Travelling, and Loving Perception," *Hypatia* 2, no. 2 (1987): 3–19.

6. For a preliminary description of natural history, a concept that appears throughout Adorno's writings, see Theodor W. Adorno, "The Idea of Natural-History," in *Things Beyond Resemblance: Collected Essays on Theodor W. Adorno*, ed. and trans. Robert Hullot-Kentor, 251–270 (New York: Columbia University Press, 2006).

7. Tina Chen, *Fomites and the COVID-19 Pandemic: An Evidence Review on Its Role in Viral Transmission* (Vancouver, B.C.: National Collaborating Centre for Environmental Health, February 2021), https://ncceh.ca /documents/evidence-review/fomites-and-covid-19-pandemic-evidence -review-its-role-viral-transmission.

8. Tedros Adhanom Ghebreyesus and Ursula von der Leyen, "A Global Pandemic Requires a World Effort to End It—None of Us Will be Safe Until Everyone Is Safe," World Health Organization, September 30, 2020, https://www.who.int/news-room/commentaries/detail/a-global

-pandemic-requires-a-world-effort-to-end-it-none-of-us-will-be-safe
-until-everyone-is-safe.

9. The last four paragraphs are drawn from Judith Butler, "Creating an Inhabitable World for Humans Means Dismantling Rigid Forms of Individuality," *Time*, April 21, 2021, https://time.com/5953396/judith-butler -safe-world-individuality/.

3. INTERTWINING AS ETHICS AND POLITICS

1. "Bracketing" in Husserlian phenomenology involves calling into question one's taken-for-granted assumptions about the world without losing the world as a thematic problem. Some have interpreted this bracketing, part of the phenomenological "reduction," as a withdrawal from the world or a negation of belief, but it seeks to approach the world and the assumptions we make about it from a perspective that allows us to grasp what is essential about the world and the accrued and naturalized assumptions we make about it. See Maurice Natanson, *Edmund Husserl: Philosopher of Infinite Tasks* (Evanston, Ill.: Northwestern University Press, 1973), 56–62.

2. Max Scheler, "On the Tragic," trans. Bernard Stambler, *Cross Currents* 4, no. 2 (Winter 1954): 178–191.

3. Ludwig Landgrebe, "The World as a Phenomenological Problem," *Philosophy and Phenomenological Research* 1, no. 1 (September 1940): 51.

4. "Woman, like man, is her body," Beauvoir writes, footnoting a relevant passage from Merleau-Ponty's *Phenomenology of Perception*, "but her body is something other than herself." And later: "As Merleau-Ponty very justly puts it, man is not a natural species he is a historical idea. Woman is not a completed reality, but rather a becoming, and it is in her becoming that she should be compared to man; that is to say her possibilities should be defined." Simone de Beauvoir, *The Second Sex*, ed. and trans. H. M. Parshley (New York: Vintage, 1989), 19, 34.

5. Iris Marion Young, "Throwing Like a Girl: A Phenomenology of Feminine Body Comportment Motility and Spatiality," *Human Studies* 3, no. 2 (April 1980): 137–156.

6. See Lisa Guenther, *Solitary Confinement: Social Death and Its Afterlives* (Minneapolis: University of Minnesota Press, 2012).

7. Guenther, *Solitary Confinement*, xiii.

8. Lisa Guenther, "The Biopolitics of Starvation in California Prisons," *Society + Space*, August 2, 2013, https://www.societyandspace.org/articles/the-biopolitics-of-starvation-in-california-prisons.
9. See Angela Y. Davis, Gina Dent, Erica R. Meiners, and Beth E. Richie, *Abolition. Feminism. Now.* (Chicago: Haymarket, 2021); and *Critical Resistance*, the social movement and journal that has documented and promoted abolition feminism since 1979.
10. Lisa Guenther, "Six Senses of Critique for Critical Phenomenology," *Puncta* 4, no. 2 (2021): 16.
11. Gayle Salamon, "What's Critical About Critical Phenomenology?" *Puncta, A Journal of Critical Phenomenology* 1, no. 1 (2018).
12. Foucault, as cited in Salamon, "What's Critical About Critical Phenomenology?"; also quoted in Arnold I. Davidson, "Structures and Strategies of Discourse: Remarks Toward a History of Foucault's Philosophy of Language." In *Foucault and His Interlocutors*, ed. by Arnold I. Davidson, 1–20 (Chicago: University of Chicago Press, 1997), 2.
13. Gail Weiss, Ann V. Murphy, and Gayle Salamon, eds., *50 Concepts for a Critical Phenomenology* (Evanston, Ill: Northwestern University Press, 2019).
14. Frode Kjosavik, Christian Beyer, and Christel Fricke, eds., *Husserl's Phenomenology of Intersubjectivity: Historical Interpretations and Contemporary Applications* (New York: Routledge, 2019).
15. Denise Ferreira da Silva, "On Difference Without Separability," *Issuu*, November 17, 2016, https://issuu.com/amilcarpacker/docs/denise_ferreira_da_silva.
16. Stephen J. Smith, "Gesture, Landscape and Embrace: A Phenomenological Analysis of Elemental Motions," *Indo-Pacific Journal of Phenomenology* 6, no. 1 (2006): 1–10, http://dx.doi.org/10.1080/20797222.2006.11433914.
17. In "The History of the Concept of Intentionality," Tim Crane writes that "intentio," the root of intentionality, was

> used by scholastic philosophers of the thirteenth and fourteenth centuries as a technical term for a concept. This technical term was a translation of two Arabic terms: *ma' qul*, Al-Farabi's translation of the Greek *noema*; and *ma' na*, Avicenna's term for what is before the mind in thought (see al-Farabi §3; Ibn Sina §3). In this context, the terms *noema, ma' qul, ma' na* and *intentio* can be considered broadly synonymous: they are all intended as terms for concepts, notions or whatever

it is which is before the mind in thought (see Knudsen 1982). Scholars translate *intentio* into English as 'intention'—but it should be borne in mind throughout that this is not meant to have the connotations of the everyday notion of intention.

Tim Crane, "The History of the Concept of Intentionality," in *The Routledge Encyclopedia of Philosophy* (London: Taylor and Francis, 1998), https://www.rep.routledge.com/articles/thematic/intentionality/v-1/sections/the-history-of-the-concept-of-intentionality.

18. Maurice Merleau-Ponty, *Humanism and Terror: The Communist Problem*, trans. John O'Neill (New Brunswick, N.J.: Transaction, 2000); see also Gail Weiss, "Phenomenology and Race (or Racializing Phenomenology)," in *The Routledge Companion to Philosophy of Race*, ed. Paul C. Taylor, Linda Martín Alcoff, and Luvell Abderson (Abingdon, U.K.: Routledge, 2017).

19. Franz Fanon, "The Fact of Blackness" in *Black Skin, White Masks*, trans. Richard Philcox (New York: Grove, 2008); *Peau noir, masques blancs* (Paris: Editions du Seuil, 1952). See also Alia Al-Saji, "Too Late: Fanon, the Dismembered Past, and a Phenomenology of Racialized Time," in *Fanon, Phenomenology and Psychology*, ed. Leswin Laubscher, Derek Hook, and Miraj Desai, 177–193 (London: Routledge, 2021).

20. See Fred Moten, "The Blur and Breathe Books," in *Consent Not to Be a Single Being* (Durham, N.C.: Duke University Press, 2017).

21. See Catherine Clune-Taylor, "Is Sex Socially Constructed?," in *The Routledge Handbook of Feminist Philosophy of Science*, ed. Sharon L. Crasnow and Kristen Intemann (London: Routledge, 2021). See also Ruthie Gilmore's discussion in *Golden Gulag: Prisons, Surplus, Crisis, and Opposition in Globalizing California* (Berkeley: University of California Press, 2007), where she defines racism as "the state-sanctioned or extralegal production and exploitation of group-differentiated vulnerability to premature death" (28). These insights are crucial to the field of social epidemiology.

22. Karl Marx, "Economic and Philosophic Manuscripts of 1844," in *Karl Marx / Frederick Engels Collected Works*, vol. 3, trans. Martin Milligan and Dirk Struik, 229–376 (New York: International Publishers, 1975).

23. Bruno Latour, *Facing Gaia: Eight Lectures on the New Climatic Regime*, trans. Catherine Porter (Malden, Mass.: Polity, 2017); Isabelle Stengers, *In Catastrophic Times: Resisting the Coming Barbarism*, trans. Andrew Goffey (London: Open Humanities Press, with Meson Press, 2015); and Donna J. Haraway, "Tentacular Thinking," in *Staying with the Trouble:*

Making Kin in the Chthulucene (Durham, N.C.: Duke University Press, 2016), 30–57.

24. On human capital, see Michel Feher, "Self-Appreciation; or, The Aspirations of Human Capital," trans. Ivan Ascher, *Public Culture* 21, no. 1 (Winter 2009): 21–41.

25. See the Race and Climate Reading List, https://takeclimateaction.uk /resources/race-and-climate-reading-list.

4. GRIEVABILITY FOR THE LIVING

1. Judith Butler, *The Force of Nonviolence: An Ethico-Political Bind* (London: Verso, 2020).

2. Sigmund Freud, "Mourning and Melancholia," in *The Standard Edition of the Complete Psychological Works of Sigmund Freud*, vol. 14, trans. James Strachey (London: Hogarth, 1957), 255.

3. Judith Butler, *Gender Trouble: Feminism and the Subversion on Identity* (New York: Routledge, 1990), 73–84.

4. Butler, *Gender Trouble*, 88.

5. Alexander Mitscherlich and Margarete Mitscherlich, *The Inability to Mourn: Principles of Collective Behavior*, trans. Beverley R. Placzek (New York: Grove, 1975).

6. Judith Butler, *Precarious Life: The Powers of Mourning and Violence* (London: Verso, 2004); and Judith Butler, *Frames of War: When Is Life Grievable?* (London: Verso, 2009).

7. Jacques Derrida, "The 'World' of the Enlightenment to Come (Exception, Calculation, Sovereignty)," trans. Pascale-Anne Brault and Michael Naas, *Research in Phenomenology* 33 (2003): 25.

8. See Immanuel Kant, *The Metaphysics of Morals*, ed. and trans. Mary Gregor (Cambridge: Cambridge University Press, 1996), 6:318–6:320, 6:311–6:335.

9. Cf. Judith Butler, "Hannah Arendt's Death Sentences," *Comparative Literature Studies* 48, no. 3 (2011): 280–295.

POSTSCRIPT

1. Verónica Gago, *Feminist International: How to Change Everything*, trans. Liz Mason-Deese (London: Verso, 2020).

2. Gago, *Feminist International*, 44.

3. Gago, *Feminist International*, 155.
4. Dean Spade, *Mutual Aid: Building Solidarity During This Crisis (and the Next)* (London: Verso, 2020).
5. The Care Collective, Andreas Chatzidakis, Jamie Hakim, Jo Littler, Catherine Rottenberg, and Lynne Segal, *The Care Manifesto: The Politics of Interdependence* (London: Verso, 2020).
6. See Catherine Rottenberg and Lynne Segal, "What Is Care?" Goldsmiths Press, accessed July 10, 2021, https://www.gold.ac.uk/goldsmiths -press/features/what-is-care/.
7. The Care Collective et al., *Care Manifesto*, 27.
8. Natalie Alcoba and Charis McGowan, "#NiUnaMenos Five Years On: Latin America as Deadly as Ever for Women, Say Activists," *Guardian*, June 4, 2020, https://www.theguardian.com/global-development/2020 /jun/04/niunamenos-five-years-on-latin-america-as-deadly-as-ever-for -women-say-activists.

INDEX